STORM IN MY HEART

MEMORIES FROM THE WIDOW OF JOHANN MOST

Helene Minkin

EDITED BY Tom Goyens
TRANSLATED BY Alisa Braun

PRESS

EDINBURGH · OAKLAND · BALTIMORE

Storm in My Heart: Memories from the Widow of Johann Most
© 2015 Helene Minkin, edited by Tom Goyens. Translation © Alisa Braun

This edition © 2015 AK Press (Oakland, Edinburgh, Baltimore).
ISBN: 978-1-84935-197-3 | 978-1-84935-198-0
Library of Congress Control Number: 2014940769

AK Press   AK Press
674-A 23rd Street   PO Box 12766
Oakland, CA 94612   Edinburgh EH8 9YE
USA   Scotland
www.akpress.org   www.akuk.com
akpress@akpress.org   ak@akedin.demon.co.uk

The above addresses would be delighted to provide you with the latest AK Press distribution catalog, which features the several thousand books, pamphlets, zines, audio and video products, and stylish apparel published and/or distributed by AK Press. Alternatively, visit our websites for the complete catalog, latest news, and secure ordering.

Cover design by Jared Davidson.
Printed in the USA on acid-free paper.

Helene Minkin, around 1907.
(Internationaal Instituut voor Sociale Geschiedenis
[Amsterdam])

CONTENTS

ACKNOWLEDGMENTS

This project would not have been possible without a grant I received from the Fulton School of Liberal Arts at Salisbury University in Maryland. I applied for funds to hire a reputable translator knowing that this was an unusual scholarly pursuit; faculty grants are traditionally awarded for conference travel or lab science projects, not Yiddish translations. I want to thank the School for its generosity and support.

Not until a few years ago did I become interested in having Helene Minkin's memoir translated from Yiddish into English. I had begun research for writing a biography of German immigrant radical Johann Most. Much of his writings have been published, almost all in German. Only some of his pamphlets are available in English. Few personal records of his remain, and only a handful of recollections by others who knew him closely, like Emma Goldman and Alexander Berkman, are available. What remains of his personal letters has been transcribed (many by the historian Max Nettlau), but not translated. Since I read German I have access to all those records. But what emerges from these records is Most as an activist and writer, not so much Most as a human being with emotions and frustrations, with humor and sorrows. We don't see Most as a caring partner or devoted father. It was therefor imperative that I unlock the personal memoir of Helene Minkin who knew Most for eighteen years as a friend, partner, and parent. I needed a translator.

Dr. Alisa Braun, the academic director of the Institute for Jewish Learning at the Jewish Theological Seminar in New York City, deserves all the credit for making Minkin's memoir available to an

English-speaking audience. She previously served as the academic coordinator of the Jewish Studies program at the University of California. She studied and taught in the Uriel Weinreich Program in Yiddish Language, Literature, and Culture. Several people helped me find her. I must thank my friend Paul Buhle who steered me to Eddy Portnoy at the Department of Jewish Studies at Rutgers University who suggested Dr. Braun for the job. In addition, I'd like to thank Robert Helms, Barry Pateman, Jessica Moran, and Kenyon Zimmer for providing information and feedback regarding the editing of this manuscript.

I particularly salute Zach Blue and the AK Press editorial collective for taking an interest and making this invaluable text a tangible product. I also appreciate Sam Norich and Chana Pollack, publisher and archivist at the *Jewish Daily Forward* respectively, for their enthusiasm about the project and for agreeing to let us use Minkin's articles for translation and publication.

Finally, a word about the manuscript. We have preserved, as much as possible, the original language and structure of Minkin's writing, including the various subheadings of the narrative. We did alter the title of her memoir by using an apt phrase that appears in it. The original 1932 title was: "What She Says: Memories from the Widow of Johann Most." A few times, Minkin's narrative "jumps" across time periods usually by way of a flashback. We have preserved this structure, but alert readers to this with footnotes. In a few places, the original text was illegible due to excessive wear of the crease of the newspaper. We have "filled in" some text where the context of the paragraph allowed it; otherwise, we have indicated omitted text with brackets.

Tom Goyens

INTRODUCTION

IN 1993, when historian Paul Avrich published his monumental collection of oral histories of American anarchism, he realized that it was going to be his most important work to date. Not only must the words of anarchists themselves be preserved for posterity, he felt, but these voices "add a human dimension often lacking in scholarly monographs, not to mention the accounts of journalists, policemen, and officials, and of other, for the most part hostile, observers."[1] Anarchism is meaningless without the men and women who embraced it, lived it, and publicized it. Thousands joined the movement, some briefly, some for life. Many others listened to speeches, attended fundraisers, or, while not agreeing with certain tactics, still believed that the anarchists had something to say.

The history of American anarchism from 1880 to the 1930s was overwhelmingly an immigrant and working-class story. Most of these newcomers made their home in the American republic at a time of rapid industrialization and a bewildering growth of cities. Many were active transnationally, conceiving the movement not as defined by national borders, but as an international arena strung together by radical newspapers and traveling orators. Three figures loom large in this story of immigrant anarchism: Johann Most, Emma Goldman, and Alexander Berkman. While there were thousands of other activists and writers, these three became most familiar to an anxious American public. In many ways, fairly or not, they came to define what anarchism stood for in the eyes of the general public (the Haymarket

---

1   Paul Avrich, *Anarchist Voices: An Oral History of Anarchism in America* (1995; Oakland: AK Press, 1995), xii.

affair was another defining event). All three increased their profile by publishing lengthy, personal memoirs. Most, who lived in the United States from 1882 to 1906, published his reminiscences in German in 1903 (it has yet to be translated);[2] Berkman penned his account in 1912, mostly dealing with his fourteen-year prison term; and Goldman released her memoirs in 1931, first serialized, then as a book.[3] With regard to later historiography, these three magnetic personalities have tended to act as centripetal forces pulling other personalities and events into an orbit around them.

Helene Minkin had a close relationship with all three of them, and often saw things very differently than they did. Born in 1873, she was a few years younger than both Goldman and Berkman, and like them, she was raised in a Jewish family, hailed from the same region in western Russia, and became an anarchist in the great American metropolis. Minkin, Goldman, and Berkman were all influenced by the older Johann Most, who was not Jewish and had been active in Switzerland, Austria, his native Germany, and England for fourteen years before coming to New York. Eventually, Minkin became Most's partner and mother of their two children, John Jr. and Lucifer. Their bond was most likely a common law marriage that left no record.

2   Johann Most, *Memoiren: Erlebtes, Erforschtes und Erdachtes* (New York: Selbstverlag des Verfassers, 1903; Hannover: Edition Kobaia, 1978). His memoirs consist of four volumes: the first volume deals with his youth ("Aus meiner Jugendzeit") and was published in 1903; the second volume covered the Vienna high treason trial ("Der Wiener Hochverrats-Prozeß") and also came out in 1903. The third volume covered his years in Saxony as an activist and Member of Parliament ("In Sturm und Drang: Agitations- und Parlaments-Reminiscenzen") and appeared in 1905. The fourth volume relates his many arrests, court appearances, and imprisonments mostly in Berlin ("Die Pariser Commune vor den Berliner Gerichten," which includes "Die Bastille am Plötzensee") and was published posthumously in March 1907.

3   Alexander Berkman, *Prison Memoirs of an Anarchist* (New York: Mother Earth Publishing Association, 1912); Emma Goldman, *Living My Life*, vol. 1 (New York: Alfred Knopf, 1931), vol. 2 (New York: Garden City Publishing Co., 1934). Other important memoirs include those of Austrian anarchist Josef Peukert and Jewish anarchist Chaim Weinberg (1861–1939) of Philadelphia. See Peukert, *Erinnerungen eines Proletariers aus der revolutionären Arbeiterbewegung*, ed. Gustav Landauer (Berlin: Verlag des sozialistischen Bundes, 1913) and Weinberg, *Forty Years in the Struggle: The Memoirs of a Jewish Anarchist*, trans. Naomi Cohen, ed. Robert Helms (Duluth, MN: Litwin Books, 2008).

INTRODUCTION

In her memoir, Minkin recreates a moment when she and Most relate their life stories to each other. Hers was a story familiar to thousands of Jewish families living under the czars of Russia in the Pale of Settlement, a huge area in western Russia in which millions of Jewish were forced to live as second-class citizens. They were barred from agriculture, and could not attend universities until Czar Alexander II's modest reforms. It was the assassination of Alexander II in 1881 that brought back the cruel anti-Jewish policies that where in effect earlier in the century. A wave of pogroms swept the region. Censorship, arrests, intimidation, conscription, and expulsion from their homes were common. The idea of leaving the Pale for a new homeland slowly took hold throughout the region where a collective identity had sustained the Jews for decades. "The Jews," historian Elias Tcherikower has written, "constituted an autonomous, isolated, self-enclosed, and collectively responsible social entity."[4] The outside world was hostile and very often a threat creating what Irving Howe has called a "condition of permanent precariousness."[5] Jewish life was centered in the *shtetl* (small town), although by the 1880s many Jews began moving to larger urban centers. Within these Jewish communities, there existed an uneasy balance between the traditional reverence for Talmudic scholarship reserved for boys and men on the one hand, and the encroaching attractions of modernity and wealth on the other. Life was always hard, however, and despite some wealthier residents, most inhabitants of the *shtetl* were poor.

It was this world that was the setting of Helene Minkin's childhood in the small town of Grodno (now Hrodna in Belarus), a county seat located on the Nieman River. In 1887, the year before the Minkins left for America, the city had a Jewish population of 27,343 out of a total of 39,826—or 68.7%.[6] After their mother's death in 1883, Helene and her sister Anna went to live with their grandparents who were shopkeepers and strict disciplinarians, presumably in

---

4   Elias Tcherikower, *The Early Jewish Labor Movement in the United States* (New York: YIVO Institute for Jewish Research, 1961), 5.

5   Irving Howe, *World of Our Fathers: The Journey of the East European Jews to America and the Life They Found and Made* (1976; London: Phoenix Press, 2000), 11.

6   Shmuel Spector and Bracha Freundlich, eds. *Lost Jewish Worlds: The Communities of Grodno, Lida, Olkieniki, Vishay* (Jerusalem: Yad Vashem, 1996), 18.

the city of Bialystok, about fifty miles southwest in what is now Poland. As teenagers living in an oppressive household, the girls were nevertheless exposed to new ideas by way of hired tutors, young Russian students who clandestinely exposed them to anti-czarist and perhaps even socialist literature. Helene also picked up a rudimentary knowledge of German. Then her father's brother decided to make his way to America in order to escape military service, an issue that had long traumatized Russian Jews since the reign of Nicholas I. According to Minkin, it was she and her sister who, sometime in 1887 or 1888, resolved to follow their uncle and emigrate. The Minkins were thus part of what would be the first wave of Eastern European immigrants from czarist Russia.

Minkin's arrival in Manhattan in June 1888 and her adjustment to the big city was not unlike that of thousands of other teenage Jewish immigrants. Urban life per se would not have been foreign to her, having lived in Grodno and Bialystok, but the cosmopolitan bustle of New York must have been overwhelming. They settled in a tenement apartment on the Lower East Side, a large working-class district cramped with beerhalls, eateries, and vendors. During the 1880s, the district was still a predominantly German enclave known as Little Germany (or *Kleindeutschland*), but would, a decade or so later, be transformed into an overcrowded Jewish ghetto. The district's inhabitants were working people ranging from skilled artisans to laborers and small shopkeepers. Like many Jewish women of the neighborhood, Helene and her sister Anna found work in the booming garment industry.

Helene Minkin first heard about anarchists while eating a meal at Sachs' restaurant on Norfolk Street, a meeting place for Jewish radicals. A great tragedy was being discussed. A year earlier, on November 11, 1887, after a controversial trial, four self-proclaimed anarchists had been executed in Chicago, and its first commemoration was to be organized.[7] As Helene soon learned, the executions were the

---

7   The commemoration in the great hall of Cooper Union was attended by over 3,500 men and women, according to the *New York Times*. The hall and stage were decked out with banners and flags. Music was provided by two large orchestras, one socialist, the other anarchist. The keynote speakers were the socialist Sergius Schevitch, and of course, Johann Most who, when introduced, "was greeted with a perfect storm of applause." See "They Mourn Their Dead," *New York Times*, November 11, 1888.

ghastly outcome of an equally shocking bomb attack during an anarchist rally held in Chicago's Haymarket Square on May 4, 1886. This rally had been called to protest police violence against strikers. When a police force appeared and ordered the crowd to disperse, a bomb was hurled into the police ranks, killing one instantly and leaving many horribly wounded. An unknown number of workers died of police fire during the melee. Seven police officers lost their lives, and one succumbed to his wounds a few years later. The identity of the bomb thrower remained a mystery. Anarchist leaders were rounded up, some of whom had not even been present at the rally. But advocacy of revolutionary violence was not alien to many anarchists of the 1880s; Johann Most had been recommending dynamite for years. In fact, a handful of Chicago anarchists did manufacture bombs days before the Haymarket rally. Next in this drama was the trial of eight defendants accused of being part of an anarchist conspiracy that led to the bloodshed. On August 20, 1886, the jury convicted all eight and sentenced seven to death. For Minkin, fresh out of czarist Russia, hearing the story of Haymarket was difficult; her "first blow in this free country," as she wrote in her memoir.

The New York anarchist movement in which Helene Minkin made her quiet entry was dominated by German immigrants, many of whom had been drifting from socialism toward anarchism in the years 1879–1883, or had been expelled from Germany. This movement grew slowly and found a political home in hundreds of beerhalls sprinkled throughout the German-speaking sections of the Lower East Side. During the early 1880s, the immigrant radicals were never sharply divided into neat political camps; revolutionaries of all stripes mingled most often in Justus Schwab's tiny saloon on First Street, the premier "gathering place for all bold, joyful, and freedom-loving spirits."[8] It was Schwab who, in 1882, made an attempt to invite Most—who had gained a reputation in the Austrian and German socialist movement but now searched for a new direction—to come to the United States and inspire the revolutionaries with his famed oratory.

Johann Most had been living in London since December 1879, where he edited his beloved *Freiheit*, a radical paper charting a course

---

8   Paul Avrich and Karen Avrich, *Sasha and Emma: The Anarchist Odyssey of Alexander Berkman and Emma Goldman* (Cambridge, MA: The Belknap Press of Harvard University Press, 2012), 26.

increasingly independent from the socialist party line. For this stubborn and indefatigable man in his mid-thirties, it was a difficult yet formative time. He and his wife divorced. He was expelled from the Socialist Party in August 1880 and found himself at the center of new infighting as the radical exile community searched for new philosophies to bring about revolution. In Germany, authorities successfully cracked down on a network of cells critical for the distribution of his paper. When Most openly celebrated the assassination of Czar Alexander II in March 1881, British authorities jailed him for sixteen months. Released in October 1882, Most reasoned that the only way to save *Freiheit* was to relocate to New York.

Most's arrival in the United States revived the social revolutionaries not only in New York but in scores of cities in the northeast and midwest following a hectic lecture tour that would become a stock-in-trade until his death. With singular intensity and energy, Most who now called himself an anarchist, thundered his preachments of insurrection and armed resistance. His speeches were stirring, as much a one-man theater act laced with humor and sarcasm as an edifying oration on the relations between Capital and Labor. *Freiheit*, boosted by new subscriptions and ably managed by Most, reflected this often-violent tone. Ever since 1880, the paper published articles on insurrectionary methods, chemistry, and the uses of dynamite. This infatuation with revolutionary warfare was itself a reflection of a wider debate over the philosophy of "propaganda of the deed," which had gained currency among the revolutionary groups in Europe—even Peter Kropotkin endorsed it. At first somewhat divorced from the issue of firearms and explosives, propaganda by the deed taught that small groups or individuals can further the cause of revolution among the masses by staging exemplary deeds of rebellion and resistance. It didn't take long before some justified acts of political violence (*Attentat*) as effective propaganda, especially in light of increasing repression by the state.

Most's uncritical brushing aside of a distinction between revolutionary deeds and senseless criminal acts caused the American press to shift its earlier coverage of him as a foreign curiosity to charging him with lunacy and terrorism. During most of the 1880s, he openly praised assassins of police officials and businessmen in Austria and Germany. He was indirectly involved in the bombing of a Frankfurt police station. Indeed, *Freiheit* claimed responsibility stating that it wanted to test dynamite.[9] He defended insurance fraudsters—many were members of the New York anarchist group 1—who recklessly set their tenements ablaze to collect payments. One such incident went horribly wrong, killing a woman and her two children. Most's refusal to condemn such practices caused Justus Schwab to break with him.[10] In the fall of 1884, Most secretly retreated to New Jersey where he worked in an explosives factory to gain access to certain chemicals, some of which he mailed to Germany. Throughout the next year, he shared his chemistry lessons with his readers in numerous articles culminating in a pamphlet unabashedly titled *Revolutionary War Science*.

But Most and his fellow revolutionaries were not merely apostles of destruction, as they were branded in the press. Most had considerable experience in and appreciation for organization and discipline going back to his days as a labor leader and editor in Germany. In 1883, from his perch as editor of the foremost German-language anarchist paper in the world (although challengers would appear), he naturally felt cast in the role of director, even of arbiter, and this attitude was sometimes resented—or at best tolerated—by his associates and readers. Still, Most spoke repeatedly of the need to organize, to build, to bring the fight to the enemy. When in 1883 a call went out for a new conference of American revolutionaries in Pittsburgh, Most emerged the leading force and author of its famous Proclamation. The International Working People's Association was established; it was to gather under its federative umbrella all autonomous groups and a handful of movement newspapers. As a result, dozens of groups

---

9   Heiner Becker, "Johann Most," *Internationale wissenschaftliche Korrespondenz zur Geschichte der deutschen Arbeiterbewegung* Vol. 41, no. 1–2 (March 2005): 52; Eduard Müller, *Bericht über die Untersuchung betreffend die anarchistischen Umtriebe in der Schweiz an den hohen Bundesrath der schweiz. Eidgenossenschaft* (Bern: K.J. Wyss, 1885), 58, 69; J. Langhard, *Die anarchistische Bewegung in der Schweiz von ihren Anfängen bis zur Gegenwart und die internationalen Führer* (Bern: Verlag von Stämpfli & Cie, 1909), 280 note 1.

10   *New York Times*, November 23 and December 1, 1885. These "firebugs" were exposed as members of anarchist groups in Benjamin Tucker's *Liberty* of March 27, 1886 ("The Beast of Communism"). Shortly thereafter the mainstream *New York Sun* picked it up with a headline: "A Chapter on Anarchism. Is Most's Arson Doctrine in Practice Here?" (May 3, 1886).

sprang up in cities along the east coast, including in Philadelphia, New Haven, Newark, Buffalo, and several in the New York City area. The Proclamation invoked Jefferson's dictum that an oppressive government warrants its victims to overthrow it, and thus declares as its first principle the "destruction of the existing ruling class by all means." All that was needed was "organization and unity" now possible since "the work of peaceful education and revolutionary conspiracy well can and ought to run in parallel lines." In other words, propaganda by the deed should coexist with propaganda by the word.

By the time of the Haymarket verdict, Most's views had tempered, although he never missed an opportunity for verbal provocation. As far as is known, he never committed a violent crime, which did not prevent New York authorities from arresting and jailing him several times mostly for inciting to riot. Thus, by the time Minkin, Goldman, and Berkman entered Most's orbit, this German firebrand had piled up a reputation—at least among anarchists—of stubbornness, resilience, and courage. This is not to say that his stature went unchallenged. Rifts in the movement had been visible since the London days, mostly over ideology and tactics. Most's efforts to keep *Freiheit* afloat, combined with his undisguised desire for control, led the Autonomists, a rival faction led by the Austrian anarchist Josef Peukert, to openly challenge Most. Autonomists favored Kropotkin's philosophy of anarchist communism whereby the collective fruits of labor were to be distributed according to need. Most and other so-called collectivist anarchists believed that distribution had to proceed according to ability. Personal enmity and the emotions that come with operating in a movement rife with police spies exacerbated the situation. When, in 1887, Most's friend and key smuggler Johann Neve was arrested by Belgian police, Most lashed out at Peukert accusing him of betraying Neve. This rivalry between the Mostians and Autonomists suffused much of the atmosphere during the 1880s and 1890s in London as well as in New York.[11]

From the anarchist perspective, the Haymarket affair was a devastating tragedy, but the publicity surrounding it exposed many young Jewish immigrants to anarchism. They learned of its philosophy, its

---

11 Peukert was eventually cleared of all charges, although Most never accepted the findings. Neve died in 1896 in the "lunatic" section of a German prison.

characters and their courage in the face of state repression. And they were inspired by the anarchists' alliance—especially in Chicago—with an increasingly vocal labor movement. Two months after the death sentences were meted out, the first Jewish anarchist group, Pioneers of Liberty (Pionire der Frayhayt), was founded in New York with club headquarters on Orchard Street. They affiliated with the International Working People's Association, held meetings and fundraisers, and found in Johann Most an inspiring force even though most Yiddish-speaking Jews—like Minkin—were not fluent in German. "It is an understatement," declared Chaim Weinberg, "to say that Most had the ability to inspire an audience. He electrified, all but bewitched, every listener, opponent, as well as friend."[12]

By the time Minkin arrived in New York in June 1888, this Yiddish-speaking movement had grown and there was talk of launching a publishing venture of their own. The Pioneers of Liberty made such an announcement in January 1889, and a month later the first issue of *Varhayt* (Truth) appeared—the first Yiddish anarchist periodical in the United States.[13] Jewish comrades could read articles by Kropotkin and of course Most, and educate themselves about the Paris Commune and American labor news. The venture ended after five months due to lack of funds, but was soon followed by another paper, the *Fraye Arbeter Shtime*, one of the longest-lasting anarchist papers in history as it turned out. An entire subculture emerged modeled on what the Germans had built. Jewish anarchists set up cooperatives, mutual aid organizations, and clubs, and they staged concerts and theater performances. They were especially conspicuous as a voice for atheism and anticlerical agitation, something that made Most feel right at home. In fact, it was one of Most's most widely read pamphlets, *The God Pestilence*, translated into Yiddish in 1888, that inspired and energized much of this activism. Most shocking to traditional Jews was the annual Yom Kippur ball organized by anarchists, which made a mockery out of Judaism's holiest day of the year.

Minkin, then, witnessed upon her arrival a mature, diverse, and vibrant—if dejected after Haymarket—anarchist movement, predominantly German with a growing Jewish contingent. A movement

---

12 Quoted in Paul Avrich, "Jewish Anarchism in the United States," *Anarchist Portraits* (Princeton, NJ: Princeton University Press, 1988), 178.

13 Ibid., 179.

alive with weekly meetings, large commemorative gatherings, festive fundraisers, outings, and reading clubs. Pamphlets, books, and anarchist newspapers were readily available by subscription or at various beerhalls and restaurants. This movement was also male-dominated despite the fact that some German activists championed women's rights. Women were by no means absent; every press account of large anarchist gatherings noted the impressive attendance by women. But most club members were men, and while reliable sources are rare, it seems that most German anarchist families retained traditional gender roles within the household. Occasionally, anarchist papers in their event announcements encouraged women to participate more fully.[14] But elsewhere in a paper like *Freiheit*, gendered language was not uncommon, and on one occasion, in March 1887, a woman complained about the insulting tone and promptly received an apology.[15]

When Most and Minkin began a relationship and started a family, the anarchists loyal to Most expressed their disapproval, as Minkin relates in her memoir. Implicit in this backlash was an assumption that family life for movement members impeded the cause of revolution, softened the (male) activist, and would likely result in trouble. It may also drain resources away from the movement's activities, they feared. One dramatic incident—if perhaps not wholly representative—illustrates this dynamic. On January 28, 1902, comrade Hugo Mohr was found dead in his Paterson, NJ apartment; he had gassed himself out of fear of a second arrest after he had been released on bail that day. According to a court reporter for the *New York Sun*, no friend of anarchists, Mohr had been charged with "cruelty to his family." He had been out of work for a year, "took the money that his wife and oldest daughter earned and bought Anarchist literature with it." He also donated money to Most's defense fund by sending it to Helene Most who was managing the paper. The reporter added that "he beat his wife and children until they were afraid of their lives. Last Tuesday night he caught his oldest daughter by the ear and nearly tore it off."[16]

---

14 *Freiheit*, October 25, 1884 and June 25, 1892.
15 *Freiheit*, March 2, 1889. The editors had used the slur "old hags" (*alte Weiber*).
16 "Anarchist End His Life. Mohr Taught His Children to Anathematize the Dead President," *New York Sun*, January 29, 1902. See also "Killed Himself, Cheated Police," *New York Evening World*, January 28, 1902.

Remarkably, *Freiheit*, in a brief notice chose to blame Mohr's death on his wife: "Comrade Mohr has committed suicide by gas in Paterson. An evil woman drove him to his death. That's how they are."[17]

Emma Goldman, who arrived in New York in August 1889, was especially attuned to the politics of gender and sexuality. She had recently ended a brief and unhappy marriage, and was bent on maintaining her independence and rebelliousness. If the German movement, and Most especially, provided her a foot in the door, she nonetheless became disillusioned with their outdated ideas around gender. "I expressed contempt," she wrote, "for the reactionary attitude of our German comrades on these matters."[18] And again, in 1929, in a letter to Berkman, she charged that "[the Germans] remain stationary on all points except economics. Especially as regards women, they are really antediluvian."[19]

Johann Most's views on women and gender fit Goldman's description perfectly. And she would know. It was in fact Goldman's brief but intimate relationship with her mentor Most that confirmed for her the underlying conservatism of many male activists. What Most sought in the relationship was domestic comfort and security with an assumption that she would provide it. Goldman would not, and she told him as much. Moreover, she would from now on judge herself superior as a woman activist to her roommate Helene Minkin who accepted, to some extent, a domestic role with Most. As Goldman wrote in her memoir with a hint of disdain: "A home, children, the care and attention *ordinary* women can give, who have no other interest in life but the man they love and the children they bear him—that was what he needed and felt he had found in Helen."[20] But in a 1904 letter to Berkman, her tone is much harsher. "Helena M. is a common ordinary Woman, has not developed in the least," she wrote. "I am sorry to say, that all those of my sex we have known

17 *Freiheit*, February 1, 1902. Originally: "*Genosse Mohr hat zu Paterson per Gas Selbstmord verübt. Ein böses Weib hat ihn in den Tod gejagt. So sinn' se.*"

18 Goldman, *Living My Life*, vol. 1, 151.

19 Goldman to Berkman, St. Tropez (France), February 20, 1929, in Emma Goldman and Alexander Berkman, *Nowhere at Home: Letters from Exile of Emma Goldman and Alexander Berkman*, eds. Richard Drinnon and Anna Maria Drinnon (New York: Schocken Books, 1975), 145.

20 Goldman, *Living My Life*, vol. 1, 77. Italics added.

together [the Minkin sisters] have become ordinary Haustiere [pets] und Flatpflanzen [potted plants]."[21]

Most's past going back to his adolescent years provides clues to his disposition toward women. Two childhood traumas defined much of his later life: the death of his beloved mother when he was nine, and a life-saving operation on his jaw, which left his face horribly deformed. One year after the loss of his mother, Most's father married Maria Lederle who strictly enforced her will on the children. Instead of play, Most was put to work in the house and was forced to attend mass. He later described his tyrannical stepmother as a "shifty arch-Catholic" and a "crafty bitch."[22] Not only did Most develop a hatred of all forms of oppression, but also a mistrust of women.

The surgical operation that Most underwent when he was thirteen seems to have been even more traumatic. Successful though it was, the procedure disfigured him for life, and until he could grow a beard, Most could muster little confidence in the outside world. It was the "deepest tragedy of my life," he once told Goldman in later years. She was convinced that it produced in him "what would now be called an inferiority complex."[23] When other young women and men enjoyed flirting and dating, Most convinced himself that he had to forgo such pleasures, and at times blamed women for shunning him. He recalls an episode from 1868 when he was twenty-two and a member of a workers' educational society in Switzerland. It was not unusual, he tells us, for male members to have relations with the female cooks despite some strict house rules. "For my part," Most writes, "I understood very little of those things at the time, because I convinced myself that my shifted face did not get me that eternal Feminine, and that as a result the tables turned and my 'woman-hater' comes out, which in later years did not of course protect me from the (totally unwarranted) accusation of being a 'Don Juan.'"[24]

---

21 Emma Goldman to Alexander Berkman, New York, ca. February 21, 1904, in Goldman, *Emma Goldman: A Documentary History of the American Years, Volume 2: Making Speech Free, 1902–1909*, eds. Candace Falk, Barry Pateman, and Jessica Moran (Urbana: University of Illinois Press, 2005), 137.

22 Most, *Memoiren*, I, 14.

23 Emma Goldman, "Johann Most," *American Mercury* 8 (June 1926): 159, 160.

24 Most, *Memoiren*, I, 56. Most recalls another experience from the time he

As soon as Most found a home in the emerging socialist movement in Germany, he overcame much of the pain and humiliation of his earlier years. Work in the movement—whether as speaker, editor, or writer—consumed him. Then, at age twenty-five, he met Clara Hänsch, the daughter of a policeman, and, according to Most, considered one of the "prettiest girls in town."[25] They married in January 1874, only weeks after Most's first election victory to the German Parliament (Reichstag). The endless persecutions by authorities, including stints in jail, inevitably strained the relationship. They had two children but both died before reaching their first birthdays, which Most thought was probably for the best. It was Most's rise in the movement and his increasingly hectic schedule that left no time for family and doomed the marriage. In one brutally honest passage, Most distills it this way: "In time, everything came down to the following question: "Party or Family? [...] I sacrificed my family."[26] The marriage lingered for years as a kind of "dog and cat existence," as Most phrased it, until 1880 when they divorced in London.[27] There is evidence that there Most had a brief relationship with Marie Roth, a teacher of German descent. Even years after Most's departure to New York, Roth contemplated joining him in 1885. She eventually married the Irishman John Lincoln Mahon, secretary of the Socialist League and later cofounder of the Socialist Union, a precursor of the Labour Party.[28]

Throughout Most's life, the topic of women and feminism remained awkward. Women's rights, while a worthy cause, could not take precedence over the urgent fight for political and economic

---

lived in Vienna where he had joined the socialist movement. Sometime in 1870, Most, then twenty-four, temporarily lodged in the tiny house of a comrade who had a grown-up daughter sharing a room with Most. He soon found out she was engaged and compared himself to her fiancé. "He was a strapping lad, I a weak fellow. He was handsome, I ugly as sin; since I could not grow a beard yet, I most likely made [...] a mere repulsive impression on the eternal Feminine." See Most, *Memoiren*, II, 62–63.

25 Most, *Memoiren*, III, 27.

26 Ibid., 28.

27 According to the historian Heiner Becker, Most had a relationship with Clara Ringius while he was living in Berlin in 1878 (and while married). See Becker, "Johann Most," 27, note 89.

28 Ibid. See also Andrew Carlson, *Anarchism in Germany I: The Early Movement* (Metuchen, NJ: Scarecrow Press, 1972), 227.

liberation, he felt. He could not see that gender equality was intrinsically linked to economic freedom. Sexual politics and the issue of free love, which became a central issue for many anarchists, appeared to Most as frivolous distractions. In December 1899, when fifty-three-year-old Most was on lecture tour in California, Sarah Comstock, a young, Stanford-educated reporter for the *San Francisco Call*, managed to track him down for an interview. After hearing about his childhood and his political beliefs, Comstock asked, "What do you think about women?" "As I tell you, I had troubles," he said. "I do not like to get into the woman question." About his wives, he complained that they "made my life a misery. They fought, fought, fought me all the time." Then he resumed with a typical analysis that reserved feminism for a future date:

> The woman of the future will have a different life from the woman of the present, and so she will be a different creature. She will no longer be a mere housewife, but she will enter all fields which are open to man, and she will be his companion in art and science and labor. She will not need to marry that she may be supported. There will in the happy future be no unfortunate marriages.[29]

If the 1870s chronicle Johann Most's rise in the socialist movement, then the 1880s recount his rise in the anarchist movement, a turbulent decade in which Most does not seem to have had any long-term relationships. And so an interesting evolution emerges regarding his balancing family and the activist life: whereas during the 1870s Most was obsessed with work and perhaps fame, by 1890 he seems to have expressed—if we can believe Goldman—a desire to settle down, to have a home other than the editorial office, and to have children again.

Contrary to Goldman's comment, however, Helene Minkin did have other interests in life, and there were times she too resented housework. She was certainly more than a domestic sidekick of the

---

29   Sarah Comstock, "Why Herr Most Likes California," *San Francisco Call*, December 24, 1899. Most exaggerated the number of his marriages, perhaps deliberately. Twice in Comstock's article Most says he had three wives. During an interview in Seattle six weeks later, he reportedly told the press of his six marriages. See *Yakima Herald*, February 8, 1900.

famed Johann Most. She was a committed anarchist in her own right and believed deeply in the cause for freedom and workers' rights. She did not share the uncompromising vision of a Berkman who modeled himself after the unswerving Russian revolutionaries. She did not have the talent for forceful public speaking like Most or Goldman. She did have a talent for writing, management, and editing. After she and Most moved in together, Minkin became active in the running of *Freiheit*, Most's paper that made its way to readers since 1879. And so perhaps their relationship offered, for both, a workable balance between family and work. Especially during the late 1890s when the paper nearly died, Minkin was crucial in keeping it afloat while many of the (mostly male) comrades failed to step up. At one point, Most was ready to quit and burn all the books.[30] "Of the few who stood faithfully beside him [Most] during these tough months," wrote biographer Rudolf Rocker, "his brave life partner Helene Most deserves special mention because time and again she helped him to keep up his work, and she took care of almost the entire expedition of the paper."[31]

After Most's death in 1906, Helene Minkin was briefly in charge of *Freiheit*, but decided to withdraw from the movement.[32] She insisted that *Freiheit* fold for good now that its creator had passed away, but a handful of German anarchists decided to continue publication by setting up the Freiheit Publishing Association. Minkin also insisted that she and her children did not need financial support from the comrades. She and Most had talked about the obligation that many supporters would surely feel if the moment of death would arrive. "I told him that I will never agree to that," Minkin wrote in a letter published in *Freiheit* right after Most's death. One of the reasons for refusing any help was the bitterness she felt toward many of Most's supporters who had criticized him for starting a family in 1893, which to them would hamper the cause. This treatment was harmful and unnecessary, Minkin felt, but "now I feel my strength has grown and, Comrades, I'm able to support myself and Most's sons."[33]

---

30   Minkin, "An die Leser der 'volume," *Freiheit*, April 21, 1906.
31   Rudolf Rocker, *Johann Most: Das Leben eines Rebellen* (Berlin: "Der Syndikalist", 1924; Glashütten im Taunus: Detlov Auvermann, 1973), 387.
32   Her name was listed as "Publisher" on the masthead of the April 21 issue.
33   Minkin, "An die Leser der 'Freiheit," *Freiheit*, April 21, 1906.

Clearly, relations between Minkin and the majority of German comrades had soured, and the issue of how Most would be remembered became very sensitive. Right after Most's death, Minkin believed herself to be the guardian and protector of her late partner's legacy. She was briefly editor of *Freiheit* because Most had brought her on board and trusted her, but she was prevented from folding the paper and forced to relinquish any claims. She presumably was in possession of much of Most's papers, and the fourth volume of his memoirs had yet to be published (Most had published the first three himself). At least according to her, she was obstructed and ignored every step of the way in her efforts to publicize Most's writings. She tried her best to keep Most's memory alive by selling buttons and photographs in order to raise funds, but even this became an ordeal though she doesn't explain how.[34] When the fourth volume of Most's memoirs was finally released in March 1907, Helene Minkin voiced her frustration in a short preface:

> Had the relations not been so unfortunate and had I been able to find any lasting local organ, the many impatient questioners would have been long satisfied. Since the existence of the "Freiheit Publishing Association," no communication has taken place between them and myself, and I was thus robbed of any aid that could have allowed the publication of the literary legacy for the Most family. Whatever mischief was done regarding the Most buttons and pictures, whatever rumors about the "handing over" of "donations" became public, the survivors of John Most are not to blame for the mischief and rumors and have no other share in them than—the cost of them.[35]

---

34 See the expense account in *Freiheit*, July 6, 1907. The photographer connected to the German anarchist movement was George Boelsterli who had a studio at 201 East 89th Street. See his ad in *Freiheit*, August 10, 1907.

35 Minkin's words were included in the preface to volume four by the anarchist writer Frederick Thaumazo (pseudonym for Frederick Loevius). Interestingly, Thaumazo would become a vocal critic of both Berkman's and Goldman's depiction of Most in their respective autobiographies. In response to Berkman, for instance, he published a scathing pamphlet, *The Martyrdom of Berkman*. See Thaumazo, "Eine Erklärung als Vorwort," in Most, *Memoiren*, vol. 4, II–III; Tom Goyens, *Beer and Revolution: The German Anarchist Movement in New York City, 1880–1914* (Urbana: University of Illinois Press, 2007), 207.

The next decade in the life of Minkin is sketchy. She raised her children by trying different jobs and moving around, occasionally assuming the name Miller or Mueller instead of Most as they had done in the past. According to her son John, she became a midwife, and in 1907 she is listed as a midwife living at 4038 3rd Avenue.[36] When the United States entered the Great War in 1917, Lucifer, the youngest son, enlisted.[37] After the war, he became a salesman, and in 1930 lived in the Bronx married to Nadia Most (née Hillman).[38] His brother John was in college and became a dentist, and shared his father's interest in anarchism.[39] Minkin moved in with John in a house at 1290 Webster Avenue in the Bronx.[40] John Jr. struggled to keep his practice afloat partly because his social activism included caring for the poor even if they were unable to pay. In the early forties, he joined the NAACP and attended its rallies.[41] In June 1932, Minkin officially declared her intention to become a US citizen and would eventually swear the oath of allegiance on February 11, 1935.[42] By this time, both sons had moved to North

36 Paul Avrich interview with John Most, Jr., October 28, 1979 in Avrich, *Anarchist Voices*, 19; *Trow's General Directory of the Boroughs of New York and Bronx, City of New York* (New York: R.L. Polk & Co., 1907), vol. 2, 1015.

37 "Most, Lucifer J.," Ancestry.com. *U.S., World War I Draft Registration Cards, 1917–1918*. Original data: United States, Selective Service System, *World War I Selective Service System Draft Registration Cards, 1917–1918* (Washington, D.C.: National Archives and Records Administration), M1509, 4,582 rolls. Imaged from Family History Library microfilm. Lucifer would also enlist in 1942.

38 See U.S. Bureau of the Census. *Fifteenth Census of the United States, 1930.* Washington, D.C.: National Archives and Records Administration, 1930; see also Lucifer J. Most's obituary in *New York Times*, August 28, 1949.

39 Mike Carey and Jamie Most, *High Above Courtside: The Lost Memoirs of Johnny Most* (SportsPublishing LLC, 2003), 4.

40 *Trow's New York City Directory 1917* (New York: R.L. Polk & Co., 1917), 1434.

41 Carey and Most, *High Above Courtside*, 4.

42 Minkin's Petition of Citizenship at Ancestry.com. *U.S., Naturalization Records—Original Documents, 1795–1972 (World Archives Project).* Original records are at *Naturalization Records for the U.S. District Court for the Eastern District of Washington, 1890–1972.* NARA Microfilm Publication M1541, 40 rolls. Records of District Courts of the United States (Washington, D.C.: National Archives), Record Group 21.

Arlington, New Jersey just north of Newark and only two blocks from each other.[43]

Helene Minkin was fifty-nine when she began to publish her memoirs in Yiddish in the *Forverts* (or *Jewish Daily Forward*); the first installment appearing on September 18, 1932. She was then living at 15 West 177th Street in the Bronx possibly still with her oldest son.[44] She tells us that she was spurred to write her own account after reading Goldman's, which was released in October 1931.[45] Minkin had considered writing "everything down" before, but nothing came of it. Her life story, she believed, was too painful. Would anyone be interested? Was she relevant for posterity? "But now," she says, "when the famous Emma Goldman has come out with her book, in which she allowed herself to drag in other people and offer incorrect facts in an often wholly unsympathetic and partisan light, I feel it is my duty not to be silent and to reveal the other side of the story." While Goldman's *Living My Life* was received with acclaim by the mainstream press, Minkin's criticism of Goldman's style was echoed in other commentaries. The *New York Times* review, while praising her autobiography as "one of the great books of its kind," also stated that "for those who differ with her she has little tolerance, and her book is full of what may be called brutal judgments."[46] Alexander Berkman wrote a

---

43 Both sons signed affidavits as witnesses to Minkin's petition for citizenship. John Jr.'s address was 22 Beech Street, North Arlington, NJ. Lucifer lived at 137 Seeley Avenue, Kearney, NJ. See Petition of Citizenship at Ancestry.com.

44 *Trow's New York City Directory 1933–34* (New York: R.L. Polk & Co., 1934), vol. 2, 2377.

45 Emma Goldman began writing her life story in the spring of 1929 while living in southern France. Berkman agreed to help her with revising and correcting the manuscript, and, according to Goldman, it was he who thought of the title *Living My Life*. Goldman contracted with Alfred Knopf as publisher, and the two met in Paris where they talked about producing a Yiddish version as well. It is perhaps this version that appeared in *Forverts*. In January and February 1930, Goldman dispatched the manuscript in installments to New York. Berkman contemplated writing his own story beginning with his release from the Western Penitentiary, but nothing came of it. See Avrich and Avrich, *Sasha and Emma*, 350–354.

46 Quoted in Avrich and Avrich, *Sasha and Emma*, 354. See also R.L. Duffue, "An Anarchist Explains Her Life," *New York Times*, October 25, 1931.

friend that "[Goldman's autobiography] is well done in every respect. Some details could have been left out, but you know Emma—she fought me on every passage and page that I cut out."[47] Minkin sent *Forverts* thirteen installments (the last one appeared on December 18, 1932), all of them now translated into English and edited together as one document. Her memoir covers the period from 1888, when she, her sister Anna, and their father Isaac arrived in New York, to about 1913 when her youngest son graduated from high school. The account is roughly chronological, but several sections describing her childhood in Russia are inserted as a flashback when she was asked by Most to recount her life story.

After World War II, Lucifer moved to Lake Hopatcong, New Jersey, some thirty-four miles west of Newark, where he lived in a house on Raccoon Island in the middle of the lake. He died there on August 26, 1949 at the age of fifty-four, leaving behind his wife Nadia and two sons, Norman L. and John J.[48] Minkin's oldest son John Jr. eventually moved with his wife Rose, a Russian immigrant, to Boston. Their son, Johnny M. Most, born on June 15, 1923 in Tenafly, New Jersey, would become the celebrated sportscaster for the Boston Celtics (he died in 1993).[49] John Most Jr. retired in a Boston senior center where he died of pneumonia at age ninety-two on January 30, 1987, but not before being interviewed by the late historian Paul Avrich. He talked about growing up in New York as a child of anarchist parents, about his admiration for his father. His mother Helene, he said, died at age eighty sometime in 1953 or 1954.[50]

---

47   Quoted in Avrich and Avrich, *Sasha and Emma*, 355.

48   Lucifer J. Most's obituary in *New York Times*, August 28, 1949. He was buried at Hurdtown Cemetery (Morris County, NJ).

49   See Carey and Most, *High Above Courtside*, 3. See also "Johnny Most, 69, Radio Voice, That Cheered On Boston Celtics," *New York Times*, January 4, 1993.

50   Paul Avrich interview with John Most Jr., October 28, 1979 in Avrich, *Anarchist Voices*, 19. There is a grave for "Helen Most" at Mount Hebron Cemetery in Flushing, NY, marking her death on February 3, 1954.

FORVERTS EDITORS' NOTE[1]

WE here begin to print the memoir of a woman who, for thirteen years, was married to a remarkable man, and in those thirteen years and the several years leading up to it, was closely connected to a group of people who engaged in some remarkable activity and led a strangely intimate life amongst themselves.[2] During those years, they stirred up the world. Europe and America were in turmoil because of them. Emperors and kings fell by the hands of those who belonged to this movement. Then they murdered the empress of Austria.[3] Here in America one of their men killed President McKinley.[4] One member of the group, a young Jewish man from Kovno by the name of Alexander Berkman, shot at Frick, one of the biggest millionaires in America and the king of the steel industry.[5] In her memoir, Emma Goldman, one of the central figures of this group, wrote in detail about its members and the life of free love they led.

Emma Goldman's memoirs were published in the *Forverts* a year ago, and caused a striking sensation. The book was published in English, and all over America people wrote and spoke about it.[6] Emma Goldman herself was an exceptional woman, and her life was full of exceptional incidents. She spent the best years of her life in America. During the war, the government sent her and her long-time friend, Alexander Berkman, out of the country for their anti-war protests.

The group about which we speak here are anarchists. At that time, anarchists around the world had two leaders: the famous Russian revolutionary, Prince Peter Kropotkin, and the German, Johann Most. Kropotkin was the more theoretical leader. The movement as a whole preached violence, bombing, gun-terror, dynamite, and poison. Kropotkin acknowledged this in a kind of theoretical way. The active promoter of these methods was Johann Most. He was one of the most extraordinary speakers in the world, and his speeches flickered and burned with gunpowder and dynamite. In Germany, Austria, and England, he would go from one jail to another. When the Russian revolutionaries assassinated Alexander II in 1881, he, Johann Most, in his newspaper *Freiheit*, which was then published in London, welcomed the deed and urged people to do the same thing to other crowns.[7] Consequently, Most was sentenced to hard labor in an English prison. When his term there ended, he came to America and undertook the same activities, continually calling the worker to rise up and attack capitalists with pistols and bombs. Here, too, he went from one jail to another. Once, it actually happened that he was released from prison—after a year's time—and on the evening of that very day he was again arrested for a speech he had given.

For several years in New York, Most was surrounded by a group of German anarchists and a few Jewish adherents. In the course of time, when German immigration had almost ceased, the number of German members in his group became fewer and fewer and the movement passed almost entirely into Jewish hands.

The Jewish anarchist circles of the East Side played a major role at that time. The most prominent figures were Emma Goldman, Alexander Berkman, Saul Yanovksy, and Johann Most, who was the leader of them all and also the eldest of the group. As a specific Jewish section within the anarchist movement, Jews published *Fraye Arbeter Shtime*, of which the aforementioned Yanovsky was the editor.[8] Most didn't have much to do with the *Fraye Arbeter Shtime* since he was a Christian and didn't know Yiddish.[9] He published his German newspaper *Freiheit* here.

Of the love affairs that occurred during those years between Johann Most, Emma Goldman, and Alexander Berkman, Goldman has already written in detail. Among others, she mentioned two sisters, Helene and Anna Minkin, who were members of this circle.[10] The intimate relations between Emma Goldman and Johann Most lasted several years. Later, an argument occurred between them and their love changed into intense hatred. The younger of the two Minkin sisters then became Most's lover. He lived with her for thirteen years and had two sons.

Most has now been dead for twenty-six years. The articles that we begin publishing here were written by the younger of the two Minkin sisters, Helene, the widow of Johann Most. Some of the things that Emma Goldman writes about in her memoirs, Mrs. Most describes as well, but she relates the same history in her own manner and from her perspective. Her goal, however, is not to polemicize. The main point of her memoirs is to relate various things from her personal life with Most and her experiences in the aforementioned group: her personal observations and so forth.

She relates many interesting things, and everything that she says gives an impression of striking sincerity and simplicity. It's obvious this is a person who speaks from her whole heart, and that the author is without artifice, a person who is absolutely incapable of embellishment, self-promotion, of taking her own part and tearing down an enemy. Her lines speak the whole truth and nothing but the truth. And it is an unflinching and an interesting truth.

Mrs. Most's marriage to Most had a special, truly unusual quality. A young woman, not yet nineteen years old, was eager to live with an older man—twenty-eight years older—a man who could have been her father even if she would have been much older. He was certainly no great physical specimen: an older, graying man with a misshapen face. What kind of enthusiasm for marriage was this? This is an interesting question, and the reader will find an answer to it in Mrs. Most's own memoirs.

One additional note: Johann Most, this frequently imprisoned volcano of dynamite and bombs, was a totally different man in his family life with this younger woman. He practiced and lived free love, but once together with this Jewish woman from Bialystok, he became a totally different person.[11] He became a gentle family man to his wife and a tender father to his children. Whenever he was in jail, he maintained the spirit of this family life in his heart. He always had a photo of his two sons in his jail cell.[12] The brothers hung by a nail to the wall. Here is the photo of his two sons when they were still children, and the nail-marks are on the photograph.

From one Most there are now two: the passionate, fiery, plotting Most and the Most of his family nest. As we have already told the reader on another occasion, Mrs. Most keeps the ashes from her dead husband Johann Most in a little box. The box is always beside

her on a table. She never parts from it. We now give the floor to
Mrs. Most.

STORM IN MY HEART

My Father, My Sister, Me, and Emma Goldman

IN 1888, that is about forty-four years ago, a young man arrived in America with two almost-grown daughters. The elder of the girls was sixteen and the younger fifteen. The elder was named Anna Minkin, the younger Helena Minkin.[13] I am the Helena Minkin about whom Emma Goldman wrote in her book. I am now a woman approaching sixty. My whole life, from its beginning to now, seems to me like a bad dream. This bad dream began a long time ago already, and yet...

Often when I sit in my room in the attic and look back on my life, I cannot remember everything that I have gone through up until now, but I can certainly feel it, sense it, and see it again. I can see clearly before my eyes every corner where the many dramas and tragedies of my life and of the lives of those near and dear to me took place. The whole procession marches before my eyes like a circus parade. Oh how bitter, painful, and hateful many of those things were! It is very difficult for me to express everything I have endured in my life. I have often had the desire to write everything down before I leave this beautiful world and then I ask myself "to what end?" Who would understand me and who would benefit from it? And also, I didn't want to tear open my wounds and let the blood flow again.

But now, when the famous Emma Goldman has come out with her book, in which she allowed herself to drag in other people and offer incorrect facts in an often wholly unsympathetic and partisan light, I feel it is my duty to not be silent and to reveal the other side of the story. Why wasn't Emma satisfied with her own life experiences? Why drag in other people who had the misfortune to come into contact with her and play a part in her life? Why does she write whatever her heart wants about these people? Her heart does not want to write the truth. It suits her better to portray these people in an unflattering light, while she portrays herself in a pleasing one. And she can feel confident in her depictions, since some of the people about whom she writes are no longer among the living, and they cannot defend themselves. For example, my father, whom she slanders, is no longer living.[14] Most, whom she drags from his heights and through the mud of her story—he is also no longer living. And me: she thinks that I am already as good as dead; but I have not yet died. She writes that my sister was sickly. But Emma knows well that this is not true, and that my sister was a healthy, blossoming, developing girl when they first met. Emma knows that it is her evil conscience that speaks when she says that my sister was sickly.[15] Yes, Emma knows very well that it's because of her that my sister became sick and suffered throughout her life, ultimately passing away while still very young. I was the sick, pale, undeveloped one when we met. I suffered from *weltschmerz*[16] and headaches, while my sister was filled with a lust for life.

When I first met Emma, in Sachs' restaurant (where the Jewish anarchists used to gather), I lived in a small two-room flat with my father and sister.[17] Anna had taught herself how to make clothes and cut material soon after we arrived in America. Emma told us that she was a garment-maker, so she and my sister decided to go into business for themselves. My father and I were happy that my sister wouldn't have to go to work in a shop, and since Emma had just arrived from Rochester and didn't have anywhere to stay, we took her into our home.[18] My father moved in with a neighbor in order to make room for her. Emma brought her sewing machine, and she and my sister began to make clothing.

Intersection of Norfolk and Hester Street, Lower East Side, New York, 1898.
(Zenodot Verlagsgesellschaft mbH, www.zeno.org)

My father would visit us every day. I think it's extremely hateful of Emma to say that my father didn't look at my sister with the eyes of a father, but rather as a man looks at his wife, and that he hated me, his youngest daughter. My father loved my sister more than he loved me, that's true, but it's absolutely disgusting and untrue to say that his love for my sister was sinful or sexual, and that he hated me. My sister was the firstborn: a beautiful, healthy, cultivated girl with a sweet and pleasing voice; she would always sing so sweetly and delightfully. My father himself had a very fine voice and he sang beautifully.[19] It is therefore no wonder that he loved his elder daughter and looked at her with fondness and love. Only Emma could interpret my father's feelings toward my sister negatively, as she did in her book.

I recall that when I was very young, I used to listen to how my father and sister sang so beautifully. I loved them both so much because of it. Deep in my heart I love their singing, even to this very day. I myself cannot sing because I am hoarse. As a young child I caught a very bad cold, and at that time science in general was not very advanced and medicine was also very backward. The doctors knew very little about how to save a child from a chronic cold, and parents didn't know how dangerous it was to ignore a cold. I fell victim to this general ignorance and indifference and was left with chronic bronchitis and hoarseness, as well as a strong love for singing and for listening to singers. In my soul, I am forever singing with my father and sister, so I would cry in silence about not being able to sing with them.

I remember certain events when my sister and I were both grown women, just after our time in the commune (when I say "commune," I mean the time when Emma, Berkman, "Fedya," and I lived together in one house—I will elaborate on this later).[20] I felt anxious, bitter, and upset at that time. I used to ask my sister to sit in the rocking chair, and I would turn down the gas, sit on the ground, and lay my head in her lap as she sang quietly, sweetly, and sadly the songs that we both loved so much—songs of the Russian revolutionary movement, the songs of the Russian prisons, the songs of the revolutionaries who had been sent to Siberia, songs from the heart and soul. In my heart, I would quietly sing with her, and cry, and in doing so I'd have much spiritual enjoyment. It's therefore no wonder that my father had so much love for my sister, for I myself liked my sister better than I liked myself at the time.

Emma Goldman in 1892.
(Internationaal Instituut voor Sociale Geschiedenis [Amsterdam])

It was also not necessary for Emma to say that my father didn't want to work. If Emma didn't want to explain, or couldn't psychologically, that he was helpless because of the education he received and because of the circumstances in which he lived, she didn't have to bring it up. It was completely unnecessary to include it in her memoirs. I'd like to dwell more extensively on my sister and her illness. But first, I must go back and tell you in detail about the commune, which really led to Anna's illness.

When Emma Goldman lived with us and sewed clothes with my sister, we were all good friends—we even used to go to meetings together. During that time, I worked in a corset factory and was a very frail girl. Our financial situation was not very good; we simply couldn't support ourselves well. I used to come home from work crushed and exhausted, and very rarely would I find supper. Tailoring brought in very little. But all of this didn't trouble me much; my spirit was occupied entirely with other things.

My Acquaintance with Most

Even before Emma came into our lives, I was familiar with Johann Most—I had read a short excerpt of his life-story—and had attended his meetings.[21] The gentlemen at Sachs' restaurant had told me a few things about Most's life, and once he had even spoken to me. That

Johann Most, 1890s.
(Joseph A. Labadie Collection, University of Michigan Library)

was soon after I had arrived in America, shortly after Chicago's terrible Haymarket tragedy, where five anarchists were hanged and three imprisoned with no evidence of their guilt.[22] This isn't the right place to take up that story—enough has been written about it. I mention this incident in the American labor movement, in passing, in order to explain how I got involved in the movement, and how I would meet Most.

I began to read short pamphlets about the movement and also about its patriarch—the father of the anarchist movement in America, Johann Most—and I would go see him and hear his lectures. From the beginning, Most made a very good impression on me, though he wasn't very attractive, with a disfigured face. I already knew about his bodily defects, and I didn't much mind his physical appearance. I immediately noticed his big blue eyes, which looked to me like two great, beautiful stars in the sky. In my eyes, Most looked like the crucified Jesus with a crown of thorns on his head. He spoke German, and though I didn't understand much German at the time, I understood enough of his speech to be extremely enthusiastic. I took off my hat and listened to him with my entire soul. He noticed me, the little figure and her enthusiasm. I thought to myself: the Messiah who will save the suffering humanity has arrived.

One time Most finished a speech, descended from the platform and started to come my way. I was shocked and overwhelmed when he stopped beside me, Helene Minkin! I wasn't used to people stopping by or taking an interest in me.

"Well, little girl, did you understand my speech?" he asked. I didn't know what he wanted with me, and my knees began to shake.

"Oh, a little bit," I answered. "I don't understand enough German."

He smiled at me and said: "Oh, it will come. I'll teach you German and help you."

A whole group of gentlemen had gathered around us. They were astonished to hear what was said, and smiled. I was in seventh heaven. My feet didn't touch the ground on the walk home, and from then on, with great diligence, I studied the "worker question," the movement, and the bitter struggle between capital and labor. Always hovering before my eyes was the image of Johann Most with his big sparkling blue eyes and his enthusiastic voice, which thundered and

STORM IN MY HEART

calmed at the same time. In this mood, I became very friendly with Emma Goldman, especially when I found out that she was also interested in the "worker question."

Emma and Her New Friends

At that time, Emma had become acquainted with Alexander Berkman and Fedya, who was a painter (his name was actually totally different, but since Emma didn't call him by his real name in *Living My Life*, I'll use the name she did). Emma also got to know Most. Since I was short of stature, everyone considered me a child. I was actually younger than them by several years, and I looked even younger than I was.

Soon after, Emma, Berkman, and Fedya became close friends and established a commune. At that time, my sister Anna and I lived in a furnished room and worked. We were under a lot of pressure, financially, since Anna often didn't have work, and I didn't earn enough and often didn't have work either. I was sick and overworked much of the time. I lived poorly, didn't eat enough and also didn't sleep enough, because after work I would attend meetings until late at night. So I was overtired, overexcited, and couldn't sleep. I aspired to take on a more active role in the movement; I wanted to give my life meaning. In general, I was very nervous, restless, and unhappy with my life—with everything and everyone. Often when I hadn't gone to a meeting and my sister wasn't home, I felt what is called in English "blue"—*kaletutne*, in simple Yiddish. I would throw myself on the bed and cry. Just like that, I'd cry for no a reason.

My sister was preoccupied with herself at that time: she belonged to a choir and a drama club, and she was out every evening. I wasn't interested in any of this, because I couldn't sing, and I wasn't interested in joining the drama club because I was very shy. I was often too tired to read, rarely understood and didn't have anyone to help me understand what I did read. I wasn't used to spending time with people, and I felt very insecure. I didn't speak with Most after that first evening since I avoided him, not wanting him to think that I was throwing myself at him.

Once, when I was alone in my room reading on the bed and crying, Emma Goldman and Alexander Berkman came in (they would often visit us and this strengthened our friendship and acquaintance). Emma sat down beside me and took me in her soft, warm, maternal arms.

"What is it with you, Estherke, my dear child?" I felt as if I were lying in the arms of a devoted mother. I clung to her tightly and cried some more. I answered that I didn't know why I was crying and felt so depressed. I didn't enjoy life; it was so sad to live in this world.

Emma kissed and stroked me as one does a sick child and, with a smile, she glanced at Berkman who answered with a cynical smile. Naturally, I didn't understand his smile at that time, but later, much later, I began to.

I went to a café with them, where we met other folks. We spoke about the movement, about Johann Most, and I became a little livelier. Afterwards, we went back to their commune. Emma suggested that I live with them in the commune and work in the movement with them.

There was always something to be done for the movement: helping to arrange meetings, passing out pamphlets, selling literature. I joined them in the anarchist commune.

The Commune

The commune was on 13th Street. We had three rooms: a bedroom, where Emma and I slept; a living room, where Berkman and Fedya slept on a sofa bed; and a kitchen.[23] I worked at a corset factory, and each week gave Emma an envelope with my wages. Berkman also worked (I no longer remember what he did, but he didn't earn much). From time to time, though not often, Fedya would sell one of his paintings. Emma looked after the house, though of course, we all helped with the housework. At night we would wash the dishes, do the shopping, and sometimes I would also help with the laundry, which I had never done before until Emma taught me how to rinse and hang it up on the line.

My sister Anna wasn't happy that I had gone to live in the commune because I was still so young; she feared that it would have a negative impact on me and affect my character. But I didn't need anyone to protect me because I was blind to everything except the interests of the movement. At that time, I read a lot, and Most would bring books to us at the commune. I would read them and often talk with him about them and he would help me with things I didn't understand.

Johann Most and Emma Goldman

I knew that Emma and Most were intimate with each other, but it didn't interest me much, although some things were not very clear to me. About certain things I asked myself: is this right, is this good and moral? And I would answer myself that I wasn't yet able to understand and judge. Mainly I didn't want to think that Most would do something that wasn't appropriate. He was still the great Johann Most, who had experienced so much in his life, had sacrificed so much for his ideal, and spent so many years in different jails—if he loved Emma and she afforded him a little joy in his difficult and lonely life, whose business was that?

I didn't think she loved him as a wife loves a husband to whom she devotes herself, but I was convinced that Most was certainly dear enough to her that she could make his life a little happier, could beautify his bitter and grueling struggle. I felt towards him as a little girl feels towards her uncle, and I was happy that Emma was enough to make him happy. I didn't judge her, because I sought and found the good in their behavior. I never felt that I should block their way or disturb them when they wanted to be alone. And so time went on. I was never really able to understand this kind of relationship between a man and a woman, but I didn't want to judge them.

I couldn't quite understand Berkman and Fedya. Sometimes I actually thought that the three of them (including Emma) were just comrades. When I arrived at their commune, Emma said that the world must be shown that men and women can live together respectably, even when... When Most would come over, he would usually find me sitting in a corner reading or writing. Aside from saying hello, I didn't socialize with them. When the other "boys" weren't at home, Emma and Most would often go to another room or out somewhere together.

One time, Most approached me and had a look at what I was writing. It was in Russian, about my childhood and the period after my mother's death, what I experienced when we had to leave our home and live with our grandmother and grandfather. I also wrote about what I'd read in the banned booklets and pamphlets from the Russian underground movement and those from the students who gave their lives for the people, for which they were sent to Siberia or to live in misery in Russian prisons. Most couldn't read Russian, and asked me what I was writing, so I translated it into German for him. It was written like a novel. I knew that I couldn't write properly, and that I didn't have enough [training?] or technical knowledge. But some kind of internal force urged me to record what was in my memory and my heart.

"Miss, you have talent," Most said. "You can achieve something with your writing, and I'll help you. Of course," he went on, "you can't read your own stories aloud, because your voice is too weak, but you must write."

And Emma said to me: "Words drop from your lips like pearls. Continue reading, not everyone has to be a public speaker; you can be a writer." I was overjoyed. I hoped there would come a time when my life would have meaning and a goal, and it seemed like I would succeed in my desires and efforts.

After having lived in the commune for some time, I began to understand that Berkman and Fedya were both Emma's lovers. In my innocence, I couldn't even understand how this was possible. Emma didn't deny it and explained that great individuals with large, open hearts and broad life experience have the right to this kind of life. The average, insignificant individual with his small, narrow heart and small soul can't understand it.

So I considered this and thought that maybe she was right. And odds were that I was one of the little people with their small, narrow hearts and souls, because I wasn't drawn to this sort of life. I didn't long for it. And I decided that, because of that, I didn't have the right to judge. They lived as they liked, and they weren't doing anyone any harm. Perhaps it was truly possible to love two people at the same time. I thought to myself that if a woman can love two men, and a man can love two women, it's also possible that two men can be in love with the same woman without being jealous, without any hard feelings for each other.

When I brought these ideas to Emma, she said, "Yes, it's all possible, but not for regular people," only for those like Sasha "Alexander," Fedya, and herself. My whole disposition was shaken; I began to feel restless, irritated, and unhappy. It was good that I didn't have too much time to think about the issue, which I really couldn't comprehend.

I wasn't physically strong, and I was working at the sewing machine all day, helping out at home in the evening, going to meetings, reading and writing, and sometimes sewing and mending because there wasn't enough money for new clothes. With all that, I was too tired to think about the whole issue. It occurred to me: perhaps Yekaterina, the great Russian czarina,[24] was one of these great people, because, as history tells, she had whole regiments, officers and soldiers, as lovers.

I wanted to ask Emma if someone can love three people or even more at a time, but I told myself that I mustn't ask. She'd just find a way to explain it to me so that she turned out to be right. So I asked myself, why does it bother me? Whom does it hurt? A great writer once said—I can no longer remember who it was—take no example from my deeds, only from my words. Emma Goldman worked on behalf of the movement and the masses, and for the ideal that was dear to me. She had the talent of speech and I, who so badly wanted to serve my ideal, didn't have the gifts. So I was happy for what Emma did for me.

Emma, Alexander Berkman, and Fedya—
How I Understood Them at That Time

It's very difficult for me to recall now what kind of impression Emma Goldman, Sasha Berkman, and Fedya made on me some forty years ago. At that time I was a young girl; I barely understood the world, and even less so people.

However, I'll try to remember. As I mentioned earlier, I first became acquainted with Emma in Sachs' restaurant, where the Jewish anarchists used to congregate. In my eyes, Emma was not very different physically than many other women her age.[25] In terms of appearance, she wasn't unattractive. I liked her a lot, with her beautiful blond hair—almost like gold—her beautiful blue eyes, and her pleasant, friendly smile. She was short and heavyset. There was only one thing about her looks I didn't like: the corners of her mouth were slightly turned down. She was very friendly towards me, and I quickly became attached to her.

During the time we lived together in our two-room flat, where she and my sister Anna sewed clothes (when they had sewing work), I was rarely at home because I was working in the corset factory. At Sachs' restaurant, Emma had gotten to know Sasha (Berkman), and through her, Anna and I also became acquainted with him. Berkman and Emma were soon close friends, but I rarely saw him, because I wasn't home during the day and we'd all go to meetings in the evening. There, we as good as disappeared from each other, because we were all preoccupied with the speakers.

Emma and Berkman were always together, and my sister Anna was often with them, so I would often find myself alone at meetings. But we'd all go home together, and Emma would draw me close to her, like an older sister would a much younger one. In general, they related to me like a young child. This hurt my feelings, so I pulled away from them a bit.

At that time I didn't find Berkman very different from the other young people I knew, though I must say that he was very serious when he'd speak about our ideal and the movement. Even then, he was advocating that one must relinquish body and soul for the ideal and for humanity, and be ready to make the greatest sacrifices. I was in complete agreement; I felt the same.

However, I couldn't imagine then that Berkman would actually be ready to do something that demanded a huge sacrifice on his part. I must admit that, as I said earlier, as a fifteen-year-old I generally didn't understand people and life. Later I learned that I'd been mistaken in my perception of Berkman, and quite the opposite was true. No, I couldn't then imagine that this pale, lean young man

Alexander (Sasha) Berkman around 1892.
(Joseph A. Labadie Collection, University of Michigan Library)

with the ever-present sarcastic smile on his thick lips, would soon play such a huge role in our struggle; that he would be so courageous and so ready to make the greatest sacrifice—his young life. That he didn't pay with his life for shooting steel magnate Henry Clay Frick during the historic Homestead, Pennsylvania strike doesn't matter: he sacrificed his life.

My interactions with Berkman were friendly, but also very cold and restrained. Something of a wall stood between me and all three of them: Berkman, Emma, and Fedya. I still don't know who put up this wall. Perhaps I did it myself.

Fedya was also very serious in his beliefs, and gave the impression that he was ready to do anything for his ideal. Emma used to call Fedya "Rakhmetov,"[26] which was the name of the hero in Chernyshevsky's famous novel, *What Is To Be Done?* The character, Rakhmetov, was a Russian nihilist with a strong, heroic character. I couldn't see this kind of heroism in Fedya, but Emma had such a strong influence on me that I began to see it. Fedya was quiet, and his intense, near-sighted eyes made him seem a strange person who kept his ideas inside and who thought a lot more than he spoke. I imagined that he was thinking about the great deeds he was ready to do with the same heroism as the Russian nihilists, but it now occurs to me that he was more of an artist than an idealist. I think that he was more interested in Emma the woman than in Emma the idealist who was a strong influence on him. It turned out that he really wasn't built from the same stuff as Berkman, since at the first opportunity, he turned away from the movement and surrendered himself solely to his art—his painting—and to his private family life.

Both Fedya and Sasha were students of the Russian gymnasium, children of more-or-less aristocratic parents. The free spirit of the American republic, which reached across the ocean, all the way to despotic Russia, drew them here like it did so many other educated young men and women during the great wave of immigration.

I'll now return to our commune. As the reader already knows, we, that is, Emma, Sasha, Fedya, and I, founded the commune. We lived according to the principles of communism—as we at that time understood communism, of course. Each of us contributed to the commune as much as he or she could. I worked in the corset factory and brought my earnings to the commune, Berkman worked and brought in what he made, Fedya earned very little because he rarely sold a painting, but he also contributed what little he earned. Emma ran the house because she was a much better "housewife" than the rest of us. She had already been married and ran a household with her husband in Rochester.

The bond between Emma and Most grew with each day. He recognized that she had the talent of speech and took it upon himself to help Emma develop as a speaker. He gave her many opportunities to participate in discussions, as well as the necessary books, so she was very busy with reading and studying. The rest of us at the commune saw that she needed to have more time, so we helped her with a lot of the housework. I was overjoyed that Emma was going to speak to the people; she would help the movement in the greatest, most important way. I didn't feel that I had the talent of speech, so I was happy that others would do what I was incapable of doing. Thus was life in our first New York commune on 13th Street.

Fedya and Sasha were good friends—companions and comrades. They acted friendly, like brothers, and yet one noticed something strained between them. It was unmistakable. On the inside, deep in their hearts, they were a little jealous of each other because of Emma. Once in a while they would fight openly, but would quickly suppress their jealousy. Yes, they both stifled their jealousy because it wasn't appropriate to show it. Jealousy was in opposition to the ideal of free love, so, as they say, Sasha and Fedya held it inside.

I wanted to live in the commune because of my ideals and in order to be near those who were prepared to give up everything for the movement, but I sensed that something was not completely right there. It felt that the others thought they were doing me favor by having me there, as if they were lowering themselves to me from their heights, like a sacrifice of their time. They were tolerating me, I thought.

So, I lived with them but also pulled away. I was still young and inexperienced and wasn't able to judge the entire situation—all that my eyes had seen—and that's why I stayed in the commune. I hoped that when I was older and more experienced, I'd be capable of better and more clearly understanding this way of life, and I'd know what to do with myself and with my new friends.

There were evenings when I got a real spiritual pleasure from the commune. For example, after we had eaten supper and washed the dishes, Emma would recite for us from Freiligrath's "Revolution," Heine's "The Weaver," and freedom songs from Most and others.[27] Berkman would also recite. I'd listen closely to all of it. My imagination would carry me to the revolutionary battlefield, far, far away from my communist friends. At these times, my eyes would wander over our kitchen walls to the Russian people in their underground cellars. In my imagination I took part in the heroic activities from revolutionary history. I recall accompanying Emma to the meeting where she gave her first lecture. I loved her so much just then that I would have given up my heart and soul to her, if she'd wanted me to.

Life in the commune also generated painful moments; a worm would force its way into my heart and begin to eat it. As a result, I'd start to separate myself from everyone and would sit quietly in a corner, thinking or writing. When Most would visit, he'd pause beside me and speak so nicely and genuinely that my heart would be okay, and the commune would once again become beloved and dear to me.

The New Commune in New Haven

In New Haven, we rented a place with several rooms.[28] This apartment had a big kitchen, which also served as a living room and home to the tailoring business—the sewing machine was there. The other large room was Emma and Berkman's bedroom. I should note that, at that time, they were living openly as man and wife. In that room, there was a big bed, a table, a bookcase, a dresser that stood directly opposite the bed, and a few chairs. Over by the kitchen was a little room that Fedya used as his bedroom and workspace, a studio where he'd paint. In the big bedroom, narrow steps led up to the attic, where my sister and I slept.

We told the landlord we were a family: Emma and Berkman were husband and wife, Anna was Emma's sister, I was Berkman's sister, and Fedya was Emma's cousin. This is how we arranged it. Emma and I would go to work at the corset factory, because it was going to take a while before there was enough tailoring work coming in to sustain Emma and Anna's working at home. As I said,

Berkman earned a little, and Fedya rarely did, except when he sold one of his works. By herself, Anna could handle the little sewing that was beginning to come in, and besides that, she took care of the house. When Emma came home from work, the house would already be in excellent shape. Anna was a capable tailor by herself, but sometimes she and Emma would deliberate about style and such things. We all laughed at that. Emma taught us how to cook and we all helped out around the house. Emma didn't work long with me in the corset factory.

Emma Becomes Jealous of My Sister, and Causes a Scene

Emma Goldman, the great, liberated woman who was completely convinced that one could love and live with more than one person; Emma, the proponent of free love, suddenly became jealous of my sister and Alexander Berkman. He had fallen in love with Anna, and she with him.[29] Once, while we were at work, it occurred to Emma that Anna and Berkman were alone in the house—Berkman didn't work every day, so he would sometimes stay home. Suddenly, Emma acted like she was ill, and left the shop midday. I, of course, remained at work.

When I came home, I could immediately see that something had happened, that some kind of drama had played out. Berkman looked at me and smiled, but it wasn't his usual smile; it was a helpless, restless, uncertain smile. Emma was seething, agitated, and red in the face. I went up to Anna in the attic. She was lying on the bed with a bad headache, and was very pale and looked like a corpse. I sat down next to her and she told me everything: Emma had come in right after Berkman declared his love for Anna—a love that was totally different than his love for Emma. It was a love that was young and innocent. Did he have a right to such a love? That was another question. Anna confessed that she loved him too and they sealed their mutual love with a kiss. It was right at that moment that Emma walked in. She made a scene. She shouted at Anna: How could Anna allow herself to carry on a love affair with her man behind her back?

Anna told me: "Her jealousy didn't bother me so much. Berkman really was her man, her private property. But making such a scene wasn't appropriate for a woman like Emma."

I thought completely differently about it. It was simply laughable of Emma to think of Berkman—or any man—as hers. She couldn't consider Berkman her man, and so Anna didn't take him away from her. Where did her whole idea of free love disappear to? How was Emma's behavior better or different than a normal woman trying to protect her man? And Berkman—I wondered—where did his heroism go? He'd lost it completely. He tried to respond just like a simple husband, a regular man whose wife had caught him with a lover. This scene tore something in my sister's heart. Her beautiful idealism tumbled down from the heights from which she used to gaze with reverence, and it fell on her heart and broke something. With every day her pain became sharper. Anna complained to me that she felt a stabbing pain in her lungs. She thought she'd caught a cold when she ran out of the house, overheated and perspiring, to avoid Emma's abuses.

I said to her: "Come, Anna, let's leave here. We'll find a room and live away from everyone."

"Helene, what will become of our plan to go to Russia?"[30]

"I don't know yet," I answered. "We'll talk about that later. For now, we've got to get out of here. That's all." When we went downstairs from the attic and through the bedroom, I happened to glance in the dresser mirror and saw that the pair had already made up. I quickly dragged Anna through the room, and we left.

I Leave the Commune Again

I saw that my sister was very ill, and she really needed me; she had to have a true friend. We went to an acquaintance of ours, and rented a room from her. Oh, these memories upset me even now! What a storm of bitterness and doubt this incident aroused! My whole world, my great, heroic ideal, stood on feeble legs and shook with uncertainty. But fortunately, I wasn't completely lost. After some calm consideration, I said to myself that all of this really had nothing to do with my ideal. If Emma and Berkman wanted to bear their little souls, it had nothing to do with my ideal. The poor and enslaved among humanity didn't suffer less because of it. The struggle to free humanity from its current enslavement had not diminished. I firmly decided that I would remain the same loyal recruit in the freedom army and continue with my activities.

When I told my comrades that we had rented a room and were moving out, Berkman and Fedya made fun of the fact that I was moving out and going to live alone with Anna.

"You cannot free yourself from the petty and narrow bonds of family," they teased me, "so you must go with Anna because she's your sister. These blood ties are stronger than your ideal."

At that moment, I suddenly felt like I wasn't a child anymore, everything was clear to me and I knew what I was doing. I explained to them that if my sister hadn't been worthy, I would maybe have conquered our blood ties, but this wasn't the case. I told them too that even if Anna were a total stranger to me, I'd go with her because she's all alone. They'd all stay together; Emma and Berkman needed no sister. Anna and I left for our new place.

The next day, when I got home from work, I couldn't find Anna. I immediately ran back to the commune. I found her seated there, sewing. While I waited for her to finish work, she and I spoke about a variety of things. When she was done, we went back to our room, eating at an inexpensive restaurant on the way. Anna told me that Emma had come by early in the morning and told her that she should not display such pettiness, that our whole plan to go to Russia shouldn't suffer because of the trivial personal matters that come up in life. There's no telling what can happen in life! If Anna wanted to live alone with me, she could, but she could still come work with her during the day. Emma was no longer going to the shop, and more work was coming to the house. Therefore, Anna could come and work during the day, and go back to her room at night, just as I went to the shop during the day and came home at night. This is what Emma reasoned with my sister, and Anna was persuaded.

Berkman had gone to New York to work in the office of *Freiheit* (a German weekly anarchist newspaper edited by Johann Most). So, during the day, Anna went to work at the commune, and in the evening she returned to our place. I was very tired and disappointed in everything and everyone, and didn't know exactly what was right and what was wrong. But most of all, I didn't want to talk about it.

Johann Most came to New Haven a short time later, and we were all very busy arranging a meeting for him. Emma, who knew how to cook and bake well, labored in the kitchen making food for the evening. Most could now stay overnight in the commune—in our attic room—and so Emma was able to speak with him about everything undisturbed.

Once, when Berkman was back in New Haven, I asked him to go on a walk with me. I wanted to talk with him about something. We went to a little park not far from where we lived, and I asked him what he had to say about the history between him, Anna, and Emma; about whether he thought he'd behaved decently with the good, reserved, and pure Anna. He said that he felt terrible about the whole thing. He had really loved Anna and treasured her, but Emma explained to him that a revolutionary like himself, who was going to travel to Russia and do great things—such a revolutionary had no right to bond with a girl who could only be wife to him, who would tie him down with children and hinder him from continuing his revolutionary activities. Therefore, Emma said, he had to separate from Anna and be with her. With her, he wouldn't have to suffer any consequences.

"Anna is too good for me," he said. "She couldn't endure the life I have to lead. Emma had a tremendous influence on me, a physical influence," he quietly concluded to himself.

"All right," I said, "It's much better for my Anna. I'm happy that she's been saved from a tragic future with such a great hero and revolutionary as you."

But it was already too late for my poor sister. Every day she became paler, and she began to cough badly. The day that Emma suddenly came home from the shop in a jealous rage had upset Anna so much that, perspiring, she ran from the house and caught a cold. Her fate was sealed. She had caught that horrible illness—tuberculosis—in her lungs, and her young life was damaged. Maybe if I had taken her away from that horrible atmosphere she could have been saved, maybe the fever could have been stopped. But I didn't know. Most important, I had no idea that my poor sister, alas, was in such danger. She would sit hunched over at work and cough—sew and cough. She did the housework and dressmaking most of the time because Emma was busy with other things. Emma would often travel to New York for meetings and would connect with Most there. Her thoughts were not on the house or on work, so all of that fell on Anna.

Berkman once declared that only revolutionaries like he and Emma have really earned the right to live.

Back to the Commune

Anna and I moved back to the commune. It cost too much to live on our own and we wanted to save a little money for traveling to Russia. We had a common cashbox. I rarely borrowed from this box and Anna neither. We worked; that was all.

Berkman came back to New Haven from time to time—mostly when Emma wanted to see him and she was unable to go to New York. Once, when I got home from work, Anna called me up to our room and told me that Emma had sent Berkman a telegram to come quickly because she didn't feel well and needed to see him.

The next day when I came home from the shop and went through the bedroom to get to our attic, I stopped at the dresser, took off my hat, and looked in the mirror opposite the bed. I saw Berkman lying with Emma in bed, and also looking in the mirror. His eyes met mine, and he smiled his usual sarcastic smile. I bowed to him in the mirror and greeted him comically. He responded to my greeting with a few nods of his head. Finally I turned around, never looking directly at him, and went upstairs to my sister. Anna welcomed me with a smile:

"*Nu*, Helene, now you know why she had to send him a telegram. Oh, holy God, the poor woman didn't feel good and called him to her."[31]

I was happy that my poor sister was so calm and in such good humor. I thought that the crisis was over for her. She was at ease and, in time, would entirely forget her difficult and unhappy emotional experiences. Time moved slowly.

A Terrible Evening

The good hopes about my sister's health weren't to be. They tricked me, these hopes. Anna looked terrible, and went about pale and silent, like a shadow, coughing violently.

One evening, Berkman was lying in bed with Emma in the big room, and Fedya and I were reading at the kitchen table, the lamp between our heads. It was quiet in the house. Anna was up in bed and coughing terribly. She coughed so much that I got scared and couldn't read anymore. I closed the book, went upstairs, sat next to her and hugged her. She rested her head on my shoulder and continued to cough and spit. There, in the dark, I sensed that something terrible was happening. I called down for Fedya to quickly bring up the lamp, and we saw blood flowing from my sister's lungs. Anna was laying half-dead on my shoulder. Oh, how horrible it was for me. Sister! My poor, dear, beloved Anna! What did they do to you? Who has murdered you?

To this day, I can't forget that terrible moment. It was the most horrible time in my life.

This episode caused a great upheaval in my life—I was finished with the commune forever.

We quickly called a doctor, and that same night we brought Anna to New York. Berkman had a room in New York, so we took her there. In the morning, with the doctor's letter in hand, we tried to put her into a private sanatorium, but when we arrived, she became very agitated. She'd heard a patient cry out in pain, and she didn't want to stay there. We didn't want to upset her, so we took her away.

A Little Luck, A Little Joy for My Poor Sister Anna

I was grateful and overjoyed that we succeeded in tearing Anna away from the Angel of Death's grip. I knew that she would never be able to work or earn a living again, so I started to work to support us both. The above-mentioned young man,[32] however, didn't allow it. He loved Anna with a pure and passionate love and took on supporting her for her whole life. Thanks to him and his sacrifice, Anna lived for a long time and mothered a dear, beautiful, and talented son. She enjoyed a little happiness in life—of course only as much as her terrible illness would allow.

Over the years, she suffered enough, my poor sister, until she died at a very young age. Her husband and faithful friend followed her a year later, having developed a heart condition due to many years of exertion. Emma Goldman worried very little about this bitter struggle of ours.

My First Negative Feelings Toward Most

During the time when my sister was sick in New York, I rarely saw Johann Most, but when he did come by, I would rarely speak to him. I was, however, very grateful to him for sending Dr. Hoffman[33] to us because I don't know what I would have done without such a good and loyal doctor. Where would I have gotten the money if I had had to pay him? I rarely went out of the house, aside from doing the shopping, but when my sister's friend would come to New York, he would stay with her, and I could go with others to a meeting.

When my sister was in the country and I was back in New Haven, Most would often write to me. He asked if I would come to New York, but I had no desire to return. He would sometimes come to New Haven to give a lecture, and we'd spend a few hours together. I had negative feelings toward Most because Emma had said terrible things about him. She also told me that he said mean and vulgar things about me. A few years later, when Most and I were together, he told me that Emma made up stories about me and gossiped, but he didn't believe her.

"You had always seemed quiet and serious, so it was hard for me to believe something bad about you," he'd say.

When I was in New Haven, I used to read a lot, and would also spend time with my sister's friend. We shared a common interest—my sister. The two of us would send money to Anna every Saturday.

Most Goes to Prison, Again

I heard that Most was imprisoned again on Blackwell's Island,[34] and I awoke as if from a bad dream. My good friend and teacher was back in prison! I went to New York so I could be in court when he was sent away. I was there, but couldn't approach him, though he called to me from afar with his big, deep-blue eyes. I answered him only with a friendly smile. I didn't approach him because I saw Emma and Berkman hovering by him, and they'd been so negative about him that I didn't want to be around them all together. As I said, I greeted him from a distance, fighting back the tears that were about to stream down my face. Finally, I gave him a sweet smile and he returned it with an air-kiss, when he passed me, tipping his hat. Everyone there started looking around to see whom Most was greeting, but they didn't notice me. He was led away, with Emma walking behind him. I went by boat back to New Haven that night, and I was back at work the next day.

What Drew Me to Most?[*]

I'll now jump ahead a little bit, and pause here. I know that the reader is interested in a question that I have thus far put aside: what drew me

---

[*]   Minkin breaks her narrative and jumps from the summer of 1891 to (probably) the fall of 1893 when she and Most were recently married by common law and lived together, and she was pregnant with a son.

to Johann Most? I will try to answer it.

We lived in a tenement on Henry Street, on the "top floor." I was expecting my first child, and every time I came up from shopping on the street, or when I'd go down, I'd hear, from the stairs, how the other women in the building spoke about me. Their talking was a very natural thing to do; the only support that the poor working women have. It was their hobby in their sad and difficult lives. It was natural that they'd speak about us—especially about me. We were, after all, a strange pair, very different from the others in the house, and even on the block.

Who were we? That was something the neighbors didn't know. We lived as "the Millers." Imagine: The wife is small, pale, and really looks like a child. If she wasn't already mother, she could be mistaken for a school girl. The husband is much, much older with a misshapen face, a head of silver-white hair, and a white beard. They're an unlikely pair. The neighbors would ask each other: "why did she marry him?" And alas, they tried very hard to find out the answer. The young wife of the old man with the white hair didn't marry him for his money or the good life—that much they knew. Out of curiosity, and in order to find out something more about this strange couple, the women would come by with all kinds of pretexts and excuses: "Do you have an onion?" "Maybe you have a little butter?" "Perhaps you have some milk?" "Please give me a little salt. I've just run out."

Then they would thievishly steal a glance at the poor few rooms and shrug their shoulders. They saw great old, dilapidated furniture, unstable floors. I myself went around dressed shabbily and Most often didn't have a decent garment on him—about money, there couldn't be any [doubt?]. They'd ask each another: "What can it be after all?" So I was often in their mouths, and every time I heard how my good neighbors talked about me and wondered, I would asked myself the same question. What *did* draw me to the man to whom I devoted my entire life?

Back then it was very difficult for me to give a clear answer; it was no easy task to find the right reason. Most was not a typical man. It wasn't his body that powerfully drew everyone to him—everyone, young and old. Instead, it was his fiery, hot temperament, his young, glowing spirit that penetrated all hearts. Most gathered the entire world into his warm, soft arms. His big, deep-blue eyes looked through me into my heart, looked into and dragged my heart with him. Most enchanted me with his spiritual and [mental?] power. But I couldn't say this to the women of the Henry Street tenement house. And not just to them, my good neighbors, but I couldn't give this explanation even to my own friends, my sister, and the whole movement. Everyone wondered, both behind my back and in public. No, I couldn't describe it with a few prosaic words even to myself.

Helene Minkin in later life.
(Jewish Daily Forward [Forverts], December 11, 1932)

When I first became interested in Most, it wasn't as it usually is when a young woman is interested in a young man, and especially the man whom she thinks about marrying. If that feeling had existed for me in my heart or my [mind?] I would have been terribly jealous when I saw that Most was intimate with Emma Goldman. No, I didn't feel jealous. I knew that I was the immature girl, and Emma was a fully developed and fierce woman. By that time, Emma had already demonstrated that she would become a fiery agitator, and Johann Most had helped her achieve this. It seemed natural to me that, under the circumstances, the two of them would have to become closer to each other, physically as much as spiritually. So I was very happy and, as I said already, didn't even feel a spark of jealousy.

The only feeling that dominated me at that time was a wish that Emma would be loyal and sincere to Most and not cause him any suffering. During the time when they were close, he would sometimes draw me to him and press me to his chest, or once in a while give me kiss. I was in seventh heaven out of joy and happiness.

I have frequently remarked that back then I was still a child, but it's a real question for me whether I ever *was* a child. For as long as I can remember, I never felt like a child. I looked at the world with the eyes of a grownup. I sought and aspired to the truth in all important questions. The young people whom I met while I was involved in the movement and with Most all seemed to me insignificant, uninteresting, shallow, and to be lacking meaning in their lives. When I would meet up with Most, I would sense the huge difference between him and the others. Most would immediately fill my soul with warmth and passion; he provided my spirit with sustenance. Long, long after I was with Most, I would re-live the glorious moments of my encounter with him.

Was it love? If so, why wasn't I jealous when he was intimate with Emma Goldman? As I said, I myself don't have an answer to this question. Only later, when I was a little older and Most had become estranged from Emma, when she was already sufficiently developed to agitate on her own and no longer needed Most as a teacher and mentor, when he had completely devoted himself to me—only then did I experience a complete reversal. I became extremely self-conscious and was even more desirous of being in Most's company. He would give me books to read, and I had a strong desire to see him and to discuss the books with him. When he'd go on long protest trips, I missed him so much; I longed terribly for him. When he'd go away, the fire that warmed my entire being cooled. My light, my sun, was extinguished. Deserted, I waited with a trembling heart for him to come back and for the fire in my heart to be rekindled.

To me, Most never seemed old; his heart and soul were forever young. Even later, when he'd become tired and disappointed, his heart and spirit were youthful. I never devoted time to the question of whether I would marry Most. When the time came that he suggested that I become his life's companion, declaring that he must have me in order to continue to lead the struggle and that I was the one who could give him courage—it goes without saying that I was the happiest woman in the whole world. Was this love? I myself don't know. But that's how it was.

How My Imagination Saw Most[**]

The whole time Most was imprisoned on Blackwell's Island, I didn't go to New York once. I didn't want to see anyone. Besides that, I barely had any clothes or even a pair of shoes. In New Haven I was called "the girl with the torn shoes." I worked really hard and earned a decent salary, but I hadn't yet settled my debts from Anna's illness.

When Most was released from prison, I went to New York to see him—to see from a distance how he looked and what years of suffering had made of him.[35] I have never been able to give an account of my feelings for Most. Of course, it wasn't the same feeling that a young woman typically feels for a young man. At the time, I wasn't a grown "woman;" I was still so very young. I recall an incident from when we were all still together in the commune, and had come back from a meeting. We discussed the "woman question," woman and her liberation, her subordination within society. I also participated in the discussion and commented that I was a free woman. Berkman laughed hard that I called myself a woman: "Look at who calls herself a woman! A kitten."

I myself can't really explain my feelings for Most. Notwithstanding everything that happened between he and Emma, I still considered him a saint. I always saw a crown of thorns on his head, like Jesus had before he was crucified. I saw the huge nails in his breast and hands, and the blood dripping from his fresh wounds. For me, and for all of us, Most was always on the cross.[36] In my imagination I see Most marching with the other captives from prison, bearing the heavy cross on his shoulders and removing the coals from the fire for me and for all of us—for my ideal, for the labor movement. I myself had neither the ability nor the opportunity to do for the movement what he did. I had neither his pen nor his power of speech, neither his knowledge nor his strong character; and all he had done for me. And, oh, how I wanted to help him bear the heavy cross! I would think about it constantly while sitting at the sewing machine. One time, I imagined that Most got up from behind my chair and rose over my shoulders and looked me in the face. His pale face, his deep-blue eyes, his soft beard, and the white hair on his head made a striking impression on me. At that moment, it seemed that he called to me:

[**] Minkin returns her narrative to 1891. Most was imprisoned at Blackwell's Island from June 20, 1891 until April 18, 1892.

"Come to me, Helene, come. I need you. I am tired and broken. Give me the strength to fight. Let me rest my tired head on your shoulders. I'll rest there a bit and then continue the fight. Then I'll again bear the heavy cross. I will again hang on the cross in blood. Come, Helene, come little girl, come!"

I felt as if the air around me was filled with Most. Once his image came so near to me, and was so realistic, that I jumped out of my seat, screamed, and fainted in the shop. They brought me home in a carriage. I was laid up sick for quite a while with a high fever. When I got better, I calmed down and prepared to go to New York to see him.

Most Gets Out of Prison

I bought a new pair of shoes, sewed myself a new dress, and went off to New York. It was the day that Most was released from prison. I met up with my father, and that night we went to the big meeting that had been arranged for Most. This meeting took place in Cooper Union,[37] and the hall was so full of people that it was difficult to get in. I really wanted to be close to the platform in order to see Most better, so I stood nearby, pressed against the wall. Some of the German men saw me standing by the wall and one, a musician, came down and took me and my father up to the platform, which was also packed, and I thought that Most wasn't going to be able to see me.

After he and the other speakers were finished, there was a big uproar on the platform. I stayed seated with my head lowered. I thought I still heard Most's strong, thundering voice. Yes, his speech, in which he described his experiences in prison, still rang in my ears. All at once I felt someone grab me by the hand—it was the same German comrade who had brought me onto the platform. He stood next to me and smiled.

"Come, come, Helene," he said to me. "Why are you so lost in thought? Someone wants to see you in the committee room."

I awoke as if from a deep sleep and went with him to the committee room. There stood Johann Most. With a friendly smile, he extended his arms to me and said, "Hello, hello, my little girl. Little Helene, how are you?" He took me by my trembling hands and looked intensely at my face. "How pale, how pale you are," he continued, "how poor you look. Only skin and bones. Are you ill? Have you been working too hard?"

Everyone standing around looked at us and smiled, which showed me that it mattered very little to Most who saw or heard him. I told him that after my sister's illness I had to work very hard, that I worked in New Haven and led a very withdrawn and lonely life. "Oh, you must stop that now!" he said. "Come to New York and I will see you often."

The next day I returned to New Haven; I hadn't forgotten all the things Emma had told me about him.

Emma Goldman's Mistake

And here I must interrupt my memoirs and make an observation about a certain passage in Emma Goldman's memoirs. It's actually directly related to this issue. In *Living My Life*, Emma writes that Most once told her that he couldn't be with her because he wasn't on firm ground: the *Freiheit* was in financial straits and he expected to be taken back to Blackwell's Island (prison). Therefore he had to refuse her and seek out a woman who had no other interests in life, no other goal than to tend to her husband, to give him a good home and bear his children. He thought that he'd found such a woman in Helene Minkin—in me, that is.[38]

Oh, how logical! Consider this, my dear reader: a man who lives with uncertainty, who has no firm ground under his feet, who cannot make enough to support a family, who expects to sit in jail—this man seeks a normal wife who has no other interest in life than to serve her husband and have children with him. And this normal woman is Helene Minkin, who is twenty-eight years younger than him, and has given herself body and soul to her ideal. She will be so happy to tend to Most when he is not in prison; she will give him children, whether he has the wherewithal to support them or not. And why would he need a wife to look after him? He had a housekeeper who tended to him quite well when he was at home. And how could such an unconventional man desire a conventional wife and children?

Most isn't here, so he can't answer all of these questions, or Emma would have been careful and not written such things. Even at that time she told me things that weren't true. All of these questions about Most and Emma, about Most and me, didn't interest me much. Most was never mine or Emma's or anyone else's. He was everyone's; he belonged to humanity with every beat of his heart. He was born to [deliver?] us all. I never felt the jealousy that a woman must feel when the husband she loves devotes himself to other women or to one other woman, because I didn't love Most with a personal, corporeal love. Would it have been possible for a child to love her grandfather in this way? Most, as I have noted once already, had the right to desire a little happiness for himself in the midst of his bitter and turbulent struggle.

It would often bother me when I saw that Most wobbled a bit on his pedestal, and I supported him so that he wouldn't be pushed down from his heights. And now back to my memoirs.

My Youngest Sister Comes to America

I continued to live my quiet, lonely life in New Haven. I went to work, and in the evenings, after work, I read a lot. Later, I became very busy. My little sister, Rochel, whom I hadn't seen her for over three years,[39] arrived in America. My father was in no condition to take care of her and was usually ill, so I came to New York and took Rochel myself. My beautiful little sister, whom I carried in my arms after my mother passed away and whom I left behind at home in the red hood that I sewed for her—Oh, how I loved her. I had to leave her behind with my grandparents, in the very house where I had suffered so much. I was so happy that she had arrived after all of my and Anna's upheaval was over, and our lives flowed more quietly, gently—in truth still somewhat troubled, but quieter.

She was still almost a child, younger than I'd been when I arrived in America, and it pained me greatly that I had to bring her to work in the shop. That was the best I could do for her since I wasn't very strong and couldn't earn enough for two. Thus, I didn't have any time for other things aside from taking care of my sister and working.

We Move to Newark***

Eventually, I started to long for a more interesting life, for New York, for meetings, for more activity, but it was difficult to find a job in my line of work in New York, since the corset factories were mostly in New Haven and Newark then. So Rochel and I moved to Newark in order to be closer to New York. We rented a small room in an attic for which we paid three dollars a month, and we furnished it with some

*** Sometime between late April and July 1892.

53

pieces we paid for in installments. The furniture cost sixty dollars and
we paid one dollar a week. A bed, a table, a stove, a few chairs, an end
table on which we put a kerosene lamp, a few dishes—this was our
entire household.

Now I was able to go to New York every Sunday and attend
meetings. Most spoke every Sunday on the theme "the history of the
labor movement," and I learned a lot from these lectures. I would often bring Rochel with me to the lectures. I felt for her like a mother
for her child; I was four years older. Usually though I would leave
her in Newark with good friends who took care of her. She was still
so young, and she didn't really understand the movement yet. So I
didn't want to strain her by making her go back and forth.

Most and Emma Part Ways

It was at these Sunday meetings where I often encountered Most, and
we became good friends. At that time, Emma was no longer in our
circle, and she and Most had completely parted ways. I didn't know
exactly why they separated, or why Emma went over to the "Autonomists," a new anarchist group, founded in New York under the leadership of a certain Josef Peukert.[40]

One time I ran into Emma at a meeting. She was very friendly
and invited me to come to her home to meet the "Autonomists." I
knew that Most was Peukert's adversary, back from the time when
they lived in London. Most had accused Peukert of betraying a good
comrade and a dear friend, Johann Neve, who spent his life in misery
in prison and died in an insane asylum. Most would cry every time
he talked about it, and he was always very sure about the accusation.
He was certain that Emma went over to the "Autonomists," and to
Peukert, in order to rile him.[41]

Emma told me that Most was wrong, but Most, who with body
and soul was absorbed in the movement and was right in the middle
of this controversy, was better able to judge than she was. I didn't have
my own opinion about this conflict, but my heart believed Most, not
Peukert. I didn't go with Emma that time. I didn't want to reopen old
wounds that were not quite healed.

When I came to the meetings on Sundays, I would spend the evenings with Most. We'd go to a café, walk the streets, and talk about
his lectures. Sometimes Most visited us in Newark, in our attic room,

and we would spend the evening together. When the Newark comrades found out that Most visited me, they suggested that we arrange a local meeting for him. So once again I became very active. We printed handbills and passed them out on the street and at other occasions. For every important event in Newark, we organized a meeting for Most. The police often intervened.

When a strike broke out, Most spoke on behalf of the strikers, sharply criticizing the bosses who hired hooligans to beat up the poor strikers and picketers. With indignation he pointed out that the capitalists needed to protect their own interests, so they shot at and beat the poor, unarmed strikers. He said that he saw no reason why the people didn't have the same right to shoot and beat the brutal police officers. The workers were in the majority, and they could do more for their interests than the other side, the capitalists, if they would genuinely unite as brothers.

Most Insists That I Tell Him My Life Story****

One night after a meeting in New York, Most and I went for a walk. It was a hot night, and we sat down in a park and talked.

He said, "I want you to tell me about your life, your childhood, how you grew up, and how you came to your current beliefs. I have a feeling this will be very interesting. And once you have finished with your life's story, I will tell you mine."

"Whom do you think has more interesting things to share about their life—me or you?" I asked.

"Me, naturally," he said smiling. "I won't deny it. But my story is a long one. Aside from that, you can read about it in my pamphlet, 'Eight Years Under Lock and Key.'[42] But your story has not been printed anywhere; you carry it locked away in your heart, you little rebel, you stubborn one. I first want to hear your story."

"What can I tell you about myself? A typical girl, a typical life; not much to tell. An orphan, without a home, without a mother. You know a little about my life from what you saw in the commune, and that which you didn't see isn't important."

"I know much more than you think I know," he said. "And don't think that I always believed what she (he meant Emma Goldman)

**** Minkin breaks the narrative to relate, as Most asked, her own biography in the next five chapters.

told me about you. Tell me about your childhood, from the time that you were born until I got to know you. And from then on, I myself will help with the story, my dear child! Don't think that you can run away from me now."

And he began to whisper to himself: "Remarkably, I cannot forget this earnest, pale, child-like face, with her big, deep, dark-blue eyes and black hair." And he added aloud, "One such as you, a study in contrasts, should be in a museum."

I felt a strong desire to tell him all about my life and about my childhood, from the time my mother passed away to our arrival in America. I rested my head on the bench, closed my eyes, and returned to my childhood. Before me images started to appear, as on a moving picture screen.

"Do you see?" I began. "A pale little girl quietly winding her way around the corners of a big kitchen? That's me, in my house with my young parents. I was their second, and they hadn't wanted to have me. I came too soon, too quickly after their first daughter, and they would rather have had a son. The first child can be either a boy or a girl: it's the first born so it's a great occasion for young parents and they love it. It's the first fruit from their young love, the key to the source of a mother and father's love. That's why it doesn't matter if the first child is a boy or a girl. But the second child has to be more careful when it comes into the world. The parents are not so [attentive?]. They are already satisfied with the older child, already calm and at peace. If the older child is a girl, then the second child must be a boy. It also shouldn't be in such a hurry. So I was already a "spiteful one" even before I was born, having come so soon after my older sister was born. Just two years between us. "Another girl!" my father began to [yell?]. I think that my mother loved me at first sight, perhaps because she was sorry that I had come into the world under these circumstances.

I was a bottle baby, as it's called. I didn't nurse at the breast, but I didn't like the bottle. My father, who was still quite young, didn't have anything to do during the day, aside from learning *gemore*.[43] He received *kest* (room and board) from his in-laws, and my mother worked in the store with her parents. My mother had begun to [feed] me, but I didn't like it and would throw it away. My father considered it a personal insult, a kind of challenge to battle between us. He [scolded] me for such *chutzpah*. It didn't help; I continued to break the bottles. My father told me that one time I grabbed the bottle and spilled all the milk on myself, and then [broke] the bottle. My father struck me hard because of it, but he forgot to change my wet dress, and I caught a bad cold.

To my misfortune, it was a time of ignorance and darkness. My parents didn't understand how seriously this illness could impact the rest of my life. People didn't take colds seriously back then, and I remain hoarse, with chronic bronchitis, to this very day. This had a powerful effect on my whole life: it made me feel very insecure. I was embarrassed to speak, because I spoke through my nose and people would laugh at me.

As the reader already knows, my father had a sweet and pleasant voice and would often sing. My older sister, Anna, also sang beautifully. Even when she would sing a little quietly, it was so sweet that it would reach my heart. I also wanted to sing, but because of my hoarseness, I couldn't. This made me irritable and nervous.

I'm certain that my beautiful, young mother loved me, but she was busy with the store. She would leave for work in the morning when her children were still sleeping and return when we were already asleep. She would come into the room, contemplate us, and touch us and take our pulses, stroke our heads to make sure we didn't have a fever, caress, and quietly kiss us, then stand up and walk out on tiptoes. I used to love this and would often lie in bed and make every effort not to fall asleep. When my mother came in, I'd pretend to be asleep. When she approached and stroked my forehead with her soft and warm little hands, I closed my eyes out of joy and felt so happy, so wonderful. Even now, when I lie in bed, I close my eyes and can again feel these moments from my childhood.

I was very pale and often had bad headaches because my nose and chest were often congested and it was difficult for me to breathe. In New York, Dr. Hoffman told me he could help me with an operation, but who can devote themselves to these kinds of things? I also suffered often from toothaches.

In school, I wasn't a very good student. When I didn't get good grades, my father would punish me.

"Oh, you poor, sweet girl!" Most interrupted in the middle of my story. "I will be your beloved mother. I will cover you, stroke your head, take your pulse, and give you a kiss."

"Please, quiet, don't interrupt me. I am not yet finished with this moment," I responded to him. "Don't ruin this image that hovers before my eyes." And I continued my story.

I Am an Orphan

Oh, that terrible night when I woke to a cry that tore through the night silence—my mother's painful cry. She had woken up in horrible pain. There was a lot of noise in the house. I quickly jumped out of bed and ran into the living room. My mother was sitting on the couch, leaning against the wall; her eyes were closed and she was having difficulty breathing. She looked as if she had slept and dreamed something terrible. Oh, how beautiful she was! Her pale pink cheeks, her pretty little classic nose, her chin with the charming dimples.

My father had run to get the doctor. We children all sat around her. She opened her beautiful brown eyes and looked at us with a sad and tired expression. She looked at me for a long time. Her eyes spoke to me. She began to move her lips but couldn't speak. Just then she closed her eyes and stopped breathing. It looked like she was falling asleep. When my father returned with the doctor, my dear mother was already dead. I will never forget the moment when my mother looked at me, moving her lips that were unable to speak. She wanted to tell me something, my poor mother.

So we five little children were left without a mother. The eldest was not yet twelve. I, the second, was ten; my brother—seven; my little sister—six; the baby, my youngest brother—three. Our father had lost everything. He paced around the house tearing his hair out and beating his head against the wall. It pained my heart to watch him. After the funeral, he traveled to his parents in St. Petersburg where my grandfather had a position. He had lost his property and was working for someone else. We, the children, were left alone with the business, and as you'd expect, it wasn't long before the business was ruined.

The tutor my mother had hired for me and my older sister left. My mother had wanted us to be educated—especially me because I was so pale, sickly, and quiet; she was afraid that I wouldn't grow up pretty, so she wanted to make sure I was highly educated. Anna was very well-developed and could sing beautifully, so my mother was less concerned about her future.

"You weren't pretty?" Most asked. "With your deep, melancholy blue eyes, your even features, pale complexion, black hair, round head? You weren't pretty? Even your freckles are charming."

"I beg you, friend, be quiet! Don't interrupt my thoughts," I pleaded. "I want to tell you everything about my life up until the day we met." He was silent, and I continued talking:

The tutor left because there was no one to pay her and because no one took an interest in her. We, the two eldest, immediately felt like grown-ups.

My father returned and brought his parents with him. They were completely shattered. They took up the old business that they'd left here. The house we lived in actually belonged to them, so they moved back in with us. My father had lost everything and couldn't support us at all, and his parents were also too poor to care for all of us, so they decided that we children should be split up. Two of us, Anna and I, would go and live with my mother's parents. They were somewhat well off, so my father thought they'd give us an education. Oh, how little he knew them!

As soon as I got there, I could sense that my grandparents were not enthusiastic about us; my grandmother in particular showed us very little love. My mother was her eldest child, and Anna was closer to her because she was her first grandchild. We were soon taken into their business. It was as if they had put me in prison and forced me to do hard labor. From morning until night I schlepped heavy packages to customers, and ran back and forth collecting debts. I'd often be chased by large dogs. Once a big dog bit my knee, and since then I've always been afraid of dogs. When I wasn't running somewhere, I stood behind the counter for entire days. I climbed on the counter and retrieved goods from the shelves for the customers. Just the atmosphere, to spend the entire day with my grandparents under the same roof, was enough to suffocate any free spirit.

They were unfriendly, strict, and very despotic; especially my grandmother. When she would look at us with her sharp and angry eyes, a chill would run through our bodies. I had a strong desire to learn, but my grandparents didn't approve of it. My grandfather said that a girl should know how to write a Yiddish letter, because she will eventually need to write a letter to her groom, and she must also know how to keep the accounts. She didn't need to know more than that.

So they hired a tutor for the girls (there were six of us, including their children) to teach us how to write letters and keep accounts. Anna had more freedom than all of us—even more than their own children. Of the six girls, I was the youngest (even the eldest was still quite young), but life's seriousness had already had an impact on our spirits.

Our tutor was a young student, and he taught us more than how to write a Yiddish letter. Many of the young students who gave lessons on arithmetic and writing Yiddish were devoted to the ideal of freeing the Russian people, the masses, the workers, and the peasants from their servitude. These tutors would look into the souls of their pupils and teach them more than writing Yiddish. Our teacher taught us German grammar. I still love German. I don't know why, but the German language has always sounded like music to my ears.

When my grandparents found out that we'd been learning other things, they fired our tutor. The same thing happened with several others. The tutors would tell us about the struggle for liberty being waged in the country and about the students (like themselves), including the daughters and sons of wealthy parents, who were participating in the struggle. They were confined in prisons from which they emerged barely alive or else they were sent to Siberia.

My sister went to learn sewing and tailoring. It was just at that time that the children of wealthy parents were learning how to sew clothes. She was taught this trade by two sisters—very intelligent Russian women. Anna became quite close with them and would sometimes bring me along. They took me seriously, though I was a child. Over time, they started to bring us into their home, which was separate from their shop. There, we met many young students, male and female, rich and poor, and when they came to fully trust us, they gave us books to read as well as pamphlets that had been banned, and they often gave us lessons. They told us about the terrible suffering of the people; about the poor worker's great loneliness and need; about dark ignorance; about the rich and debauched lives of the capitalist classes; about the czar and his court and all the functionaries great and small who bathed in the blood of the languishing working masses; about the church's role in Russian society; about the horrible pains of the revolutionaries, the young students, male and female, who were teaching the masses, leading them to a liberated life. They lectured to us about all of this. My sister and I were very enthusiastic about these new ideas. At home, often at night, we would read the banned pamphlets and books. And when we didn't understand something, we went to our teachers, and they explained it to us.

I fixed my eyes on Most and continued, "Just as I now come to you when there is something I don't understand in a book you've given me to read." He hugged me tightly, and I continued to talk, like a child to her father.

We didn't speak about these secret things with our young aunts, my mother's sisters. We were all still quite young, so we had lots of other things to talk about. It was very difficult living this way. When we would go behind the stove to talk, our grandparents would consider it a serious crime. So we began to make plans to sneak out of the house and be free from the oppressive atmosphere, to enjoy a little bit of nature and liberate ourselves from the despots. I used to say that our grandparents were our tsar and the royal court; we were their prisoners, their slaves.

One time, my grandmother took an iron yard stick, which she used to measure material in the store, and struck my aunt Esther on the head with it. She had committed some kind of sin. Esther was the youngest of my aunts, only one year older than me, and she was my friend. When I saw this, I became very upset and began to scream and cry. My grandmother told me: "Be quiet, you crazy girl! Why are you butting in when I am trying to teach my child?"

"You're teaching a child with an iron over the head and you still call yourself a mother?" I said. "You think that just because you gave birth to her that she's yours? You know, no living person belongs to another. Slavery doesn't exist anymore."

I started to shout and cry again. If I hadn't been her granddaughter and an orphan, she would certainly have struck the iron over my head; but she couldn't do it, because pious people believe that you are not allowed to strike an orphan boy or girl. I felt a storm in my heart.

My aunt Esther started to suffer terrible headaches. In the middle of the night she would walk around the bedroom crying in pain. She didn't want to tell her mother, because she didn't expect she'd get sympathy from her. Oh, what it would be like to be free! The birdies were growing up at home; but they could not fly.

The store was closed early on Friday and all day Saturday, so we worked out a plan to sneak out and be free every Friday when our grandparents went to bed early. We would pretend to go to sleep early, lie in bed, and wait until they fell asleep. Then, in the dark, we would put on our finest clothes, which we had put aside earlier so that we could easily find them. Our mood was giddy. We'd carry our shoes so that we could leave the house silently, and one by one we went down the stairs in our socks. On the final step, we would put on our shoes and run out into the yard. We raised our hands to the sky and laughed with joy. We walked around the streets and talked about everything that was in our young hearts. I enjoyed this so much that even now, when I'm speaking about it, I am reliving it and everything appears right before my eyes. When it was time for us to go back, we would suddenly become very quiet. Our feet were heavy, and we had to drag them home. We'd take off our shoes and sneak back into the house and, lying in bed, we'd think long and hard about everything.

An End to Our Night Walks

One time, when we returned from one of these Friday night expeditions, something happened that ended our secret evening walks and brought a new twist to our lives. Anna and I had been extremely upset recently; we'd found out that our comrades, teachers, and friends— the students who took us under their wing—had been arrested. They were found with banned literature and were instantly sent away. Our hearts cried out for their fate. We immediately burned everything we had. We were in much silent turmoil because of it.

One Friday evening we were walking the streets, trying to figure out what to do next, how to organize the rest of our lives, and we lost track of time; we got home much later than usual. Every time we returned from one of these walks, one of us would go into the house by ourselves to check that everything was okay and the others could come up. This time, it was my turn. Quietly, with shoes in hand, I went upstairs and into the kitchen. The house was dark and quiet—thus, no danger. I was about to give the all-clear to the others, when something caught my eye and I stood stock still. In the kitchen, behind the door, stood a figure who looked as if she had risen from the grave; an image, dressed in white, with a white kerchief on her head, a yellow wrinkled face, and sparkling green eyes. I screamed and collapsed. It was my grandmother. Late that night, she had gone to check on us. Seeing that we weren't in our room, she became furious, so she planted herself behind the door and waited to catch us in this terrible crime. She considered me the leader since I would often speak up against her, especially since the time that she had beaten poor Esther. The maid didn't know much of anything, and what she did know she never gave up, as she was always on our side. A terrible scene then played out...

My grandfather was a decent man. From the time that I was a young girl, I remember him taking me in his arms, crumbling pieces of white bread into a glass of milk and gently feeding me, "Eat, eat, right in your mouth," he'd say. When he heard or saw my grandmother coming, he would get me off his lap and act angry with me for not eating. My grandfather was under her influence his entire life, and would be angry at us because my grandmother was. I didn't hate him, but I was furious with him for being under her thumb. On that evening as well, down the stairs in his nightshirt, he helped her scold and shout at me. I responded by pointing out how much she wanted to hit me, and how she couldn't do it because I was an orphan.

Right before my eyes, the image of my dear, beloved mother appeared. I started to laugh hysterically. I thought about the iron ruler that my grandmother hit her daughters on the head with, and I felt a desire for revenge because it upset her that she could not—was not allowed to—hit me.

When this episode was over and the children had "sneaked back" into their beds, my sister and I hugged each other and cried quietly for a long time. When we calmed down, we spoke for a while, and decided that we had to find a way to leave, to go to America—the place about which we had heard so much, the land where freedom reigned, where one could speak and write about whatever one wanted, where we could work and earn for ourselves, and not be anyone's charity case. We decided that I would go to my father and tell him everything, and suggest to him, force him, to come with us to America. With this decision made, we fell asleep, wrapped in each other's arms.

The next day was Saturday, so the shop was closed. The house was deadly silent, and all of the children went around with red swollen ears, deathly pale faces, and heads hung low. No one wanted to say a word. My grandmother was also silent because she had no more to say; she had already said everything and there was nothing left. Of course, my grandfather was also silent. I shut myself up in a little side room, and stayed there the entire day with a headache. My grandparents went to sleep after the evening meal, as they did every Saturday. The maid brought me something to eat. She had also been crying. My little aunties went around silently and cried too. Their young hearts were heavy; they felt that a change was coming to their lives.

I Leave My Grandfather's House

That evening, I began to pack a couple of my old dresses. Two girls, friends from the neighborhood, came over to say goodbye. They asked me where I was going, so I told them that I myself didn't know where: I was running away from one witch to another. I regret saying that because now that I understand life, I don't blame either grandmother as harshly for their unkindness to us. I blame more the darkness of the era in which we lived—they, the older generation, were also victims of those times.

I didn't have any money for the trip, which took about two hours by train, so I decided to walk. It wasn't very far. It was Sunday morning, a beautiful summer day. Everyone was already at work when I left for the little town of Bielsk to rejoin my father and begin a new life.[44] The maid gave me a large package of food, and kissed me and cried when we said goodbye. I never forgot her. My sister accompanied me a large part of the way. I really wanted to go to the two sisters in the tailor shop, but we didn't because we didn't know what had happened there. All day long, I followed the railway tracks from Bialystok to Bielsk. Fortunately, this was a direct route. I knew that I could get money to take the train, but in my excited state, I wanted to go by foot. I wanted to test myself, to try my strength: to begin my new life with my own two feet. Everything had taken shape in mid-air, in our young, fanciful hearts.

We Move to America

We began the process of moving, and decided to send my little sister,

Rochel, to Bialystok. I dressed her in a little red hood. When I looked out the train window, she looked like an angel.

My heart was full of maternal love for her. My father's sister helped us, or rather I helped her, prepare for our journey. My father went around trying to raise money.[45] Three months later we left for America.[46]

On a fine spring day in June 1888, my father, my sister Anna, and I arrived in New York.[47] My uncle, my father's only brother, who had run away from the military a year earlier, was waiting for us at Castle Garden. He had already gotten an apartment for us.

Most Compares Me to Emma Goldman

I interrupted my story and turned to Most: "Do you want me to describe our first apartment and the life we led there?"

"Do I want you to?" he asked. "You have given me much enjoyment with your life story. You've described it so beautifully!"

He was quiet for a while and then said as if to himself, "What a girl!... What a beautiful, generous soul! And this is the 'simple, silly girl' that Emma used to describe to me..."

I responded that, "she would say to me, that that was your opinion of me: 'a foolish girl.' You had no other opinion about me."

Most laughed, "Do you not understand that a person like Emma Goldman doesn't want anyone, besides herself, to be considered a person?" He thought about it again, and continued, "I was interested in you the very first night I saw you; I could tell there was a fire in your soul. The fire shone from your big and serious eyes, from which all of your feelings are reflected. Now I understand why you lack courage: your childhood, your whole life has caused you to feel so insecure and self-conscious. You could never be a speaker, but, given a chance, you could train to become a writer. You and Emma are two completely different people. She is very precocious, and with it, she pulls the world of men into her. Emma has the talent of speech, and we need new strength for our movement. That is why I helped her to [succeed?]. And I would be really happy if she would not use it so much for her personal aims."

"Well," I said, "she can use it a little for herself as long as it is useful for our ideal."

"Whatever you do in your life, you'll do with your entire, pure soul," he said, with fatherly love. "Now tell me more about your life.

Tell me about your first apartment here in America. That was where you stopped. Later, when you have finished your story, I'll tell you about my life."

So I continued...

Our First Apartment in America

The apartment that my uncle prepared for us was on Catherine Street, not far from the Bowery. There were two rooms: a front room and a bedroom. The household consisted of a sofa, which at night could be made into a double bed; a table; a few old chairs; an old commode; a kerosene stove and lamp; and a few pots and other utensils. Two little windows overlooking a dirty courtyard provided some weak light in the front room, and there was a little window, high up in the hallway. The bedroom didn't have a window. A big, old, wooden bed was the only furniture in the room. There was no room to walk around the bed, so you had to get into it by holding your legs in the [air]. On the side of the bed was a chair. We also had a few hooks in the wall where we could hang our things.

My father and uncle slept on the sofa bed in the front room, and Anna and I slept in the bedroom. My poor uncle had done his best for us, and I was very grateful to him for it. The first night in our new place was very tumultuous; the cockroaches greeted us with a great parade. Out of immense joy, they almost ate us up. We all got out of our beds and began a bitter war with them, scalding them with boiling water, burning them. Nothing helped. When they were drunk on our blood and we were exhausted from the fight, we all eventually fell asleep.

In the morning, my uncle got up and went to work. It bothered me that I hadn't gotten up in time to make him breakfast. I had pledged to myself that I would care for my uncle and provide a home-like atmosphere, but for different reasons, we all shared in this. That day—it was Saturday—my father, Anna, and I all worked the whole day to get rid of the roaches. We scalded the beds, doused them in kerosene, and somehow managed to chase them away.

When my uncle came home from work that night, he took us out for supper. The restaurant we went to was owned by two brothers by the name of Sachs. It was a place where many freethinkers, radicals, and anarchists would eat and spend time. We immediately got to know many people. They told us about the movement in America, about the horrible tragedy the previous year in Chicago—the Haymarket tragedy—where five anarchists were hanged after being accused of throwing a bomb. It was my first blow in this free country. The men then spoke of the old man, the patriarch of the anarchist movement, the father of anarchism, the great Johann Most.

Here we both laughed, Most and I. Really, Most was not an old man at that time.[48] His hair had become white before its time, but his eyes were young, fresh, and fiery. His face was unwrinkled, his movements were quick and youthful.

"Do you remember when you came for the first time to a meeting on Orchard Street?"[49] Most interrupted. "You were a small, thin, pale girl with short hair and a European dress. You stood against the wall on tiptoes, opened your large eyes, opened your mouth, extended your ears like a rabbit, and didn't move from your place.... Do you remember that? You captured my attention immediately. 'She looks like a Russian girl,' I thought to myself, and right away I got to know you, and helped you enter into our circles."

I wanted to say something, but Most continued to speak. "Tell me, what are you thinking about doing with your life?"

"I don't know, and I think very little about my personal life," I answered him. "I will live together with my sister, work in the shop, take part in the movement and work for it."

"And what do you consider 'working for it'?" he asked. I didn't really know how to answer. In truth, I didn't have a clear idea about what I could do for the movement, how I could be of use.

"Help me! Tell me what I can do, how I can make myself useful to the movement; be my teacher. I want to serve the greater cause for which you have already suffered so much and for which you still suffer. I will do anything that you ask. It's not enough for me to go to meetings, sell literature, and distribute hand-bills. I want to do more. I want to sacrifice with my life, the way many others have already done."

Most considered me and said with a smile: "You poor child! Dear, little girl, what can you do? Your spirit is ready for great sacrifice, but the flesh, your body, is weak. You are still so young, so skinny, and so weak. What can you accomplish after you work the whole day in the factory? Sometimes when you come to read with me in my office, I can see how you struggle to stay awake. It's enough that you continue to remain loyal to our ideal and do what you do now. You are with us, work for us, and help us—that is enough. Whoever is not against us is with us." And with that, that evening's conversation—a long conversation in which I told Most about my whole life—came to an end.

Alexander Berkman's Assassination of the Steel Magnate Frick, and Emma's Mistakes*****

I continued to live with my younger sister, Rochel, in Newark, where we both worked in corset making. One day, Most came to me very agitated. I already knew why because I'd read about Alexander Berkman's assassination of Henry C. Frick, the steel magnate. I was also very troubled because of it.

Emma Goldman lies vividly in her book, when she says that while she and Berkman were preparing to assassinate Frick, "Helene Minkin was living with Most, and was expecting a child."[50] She says she didn't want to consult Most about the assassination because she didn't want to disturb us. Emma always tried to present herself as a fine, honorable individual, and as a heroine. So I'll tell you something, then pose a question.

First the fact: Berkman experimented with a bomb in the house of one of Emma's friends. There were little children there. Emma said that if there was an explosion and children killed, it would certainly be horrible, but in this significant instance one can't avoid making sacrifices—even small children.

And now my question: how is it that she stopped herself from consulting with Most about Frick's assassination, only because Helene Minkin was living with him and was to be the mother of his child? Is that logical? How did she suddenly become so worried about me? How could she have disturbed Helene Minkin, with her unborn child, by going to Most's office to consult with him? Did she think that her feminine wiles were so powerful that when Most saw her, he'd become so captivated that he'd get rid of his wife and child and give himself to her entirely? And was it because she was such a fine individual, that she didn't want to do this?

***** Minkin ends her biographical sketch to Most, and resumes her main narrative, picking up in July 1892. Even though Frick survived the attempt on his life, Minkin frequently uses the term "assassination."

"The Attentat. Alexander Berkman's attempt to assassinate Frick,"
from *Harper's Weekly*, August 6, 1892.

I have a different reading of what happened: I believe that if Emma really thought she could make Most fall in love with her and leave me, then she'd have met with him and done it. Furthermore, she would have done this even if she didn't want him—if only to boast about her great power over the men whom she writes about in her book. In reality, however, this whole story of hers is false. When Frick was shot, I was still working in Newark and living with my sister. Most and I were together much later. Frick was shot in 1892, and my first child was born in 1894.

Berkman sat in prison for fourteen years, and Most was dead by the time he was released.[51] Berkman came to visit me, but didn't find me at home, but he recognized my eldest son—who looked like Most—playing in the street. When I got home, my son told me that a man by the name of Alexander Berkman had been around. He'd spoken with him, said that his father was a great man, and that he, my son, would grow up to be as great as his father. My son was then about eleven years old.

✦ ✦

Now, back to Frick's assassination: As I already mentioned, Most came to me in Newark immediately after the assassination both agitated and in despair. In his opinion, Frick's assassination dealt a heavy blow to the movement; we could expect a strong reaction because of it.

"This is a precious thing for the capitalist classes," Most said to me bitterly. "The capitalists will now begin anarchist-baiting and it will hinder our work. They'll vent their anger entirely on Berkman. If he was an American worker, perhaps it would have had a useful impact; but Berkman is a Russian Jew, a 'foreigner.' Even the American workers will take their hatred for Frick out on Berkman.[52] They will now appear sympathetic to Frick. So it is with workers in general, but the American worker especially." Most was furious: "Why didn't they consult me? I would have explained the situation to them. I'm an old veteran in the movement, and know that everything has its time and its place, and this assassination was not appropriate."

A Few Questions For Emma Goldman

Emma said that Most hated Berkman because he was jealous of him. This is laughable and even petty. If this had really been the case, Most wouldn't have taken Berkman on at *Freiheit* so that he could learn typesetting and wouldn't have given him a position. It was precisely the opposite: Berkman was probably jealous of Most. But why did Emma write at all about the issue of jealousy? Why did she have to mix personal lives with the ideal? Why air dirty laundry in public? Perhaps it's titillating to read these kinds of things in a book: intimate, personal things about life excite the reader. But it's harmful to the movement. If a little bit of her past spirit of sacrifice remained in Emma's heart, she would have left these very intimate descriptions out of her book. In her life story, why did she have to include people who had the misfortune of coming into contact with her? Why didn't she, with her great physical enchantments, just completely remove me, poor Helene Minkin, instead of—at every suitable or rather unsuitable opportunity—showing her contempt for, her hatred toward me? Why did she even admit that Most was interested in Helene Minkin? With regards to Berkman's act, she said that Most had shown himself to be a chicken; to protect his own skin he hadn't spoken out with open enthusiasm toward the act or to Berkman—to say this is neither fine nor honorable.[53] So Most had his entire life, from his childhood on, behaved like a coward, like someone protecting his own hide? If Most distanced himself from Berkman's deed, he had his reasons for it. He found it necessary to retreat from what Berkman did. Most was like the general of a great army; he knew well how to act in this kind of situation. He lived his life alone. He didn't enjoy the privileges of a charming, fascinating woman. No one supported him. No one had bought him gold watches or velvet clothing. No one had sent him to Europe to study. No one had earmarked a hundred for him. He didn't travel with a manager for years on the coffers of the poor workers who gave their few pennies to the movement.[54] Most didn't spend all his money on prostitutes. He didn't give it to his sister or brother. He struggled bitterly and worked hard. To the end of his life, he labored.

In her book, Emma further said that Most sought to influence Henry Bauer not to follow in Berkman's footsteps.[55] She said that Most encouraged Bauer to go to Pittsburgh and search through Berkman's things when he was asleep. If he found something suspicious, which would prove that Berkman had come to carry out a terrorist act, he should shoot him in his sleep like a dog. And Bauer had actually taken a revolver with him to do what Most ordered. They planned to kill Berkman. Can there be anything more laughable and hateful than this? Apparently, Emma doesn't understand her readers if she believes that they would swallow this.

And even further, Emma wrote that she needed a few dollars for the Berkman-assassination. To that end, she worked out a plan in which she would sell herself in the street—and really why not? What wouldn't a revolutionary do for her ideal? Is it possible that she couldn't get a few dollars from the other comrades in a time of need? Where were Fedya and all her other close friends? She had to go sell herself? And she got so lucky, she says, that the man she encountered gave her ten dollars, just like that, because he immediately saw that she was not experienced in the business. By my life, such luck! This man could have been a bad one who wouldn't have given ten dollars for nothing. [...] and her sister Helena sent her money. She went to Peukert, the "autonomist," told him what she was going to do and begged him to help. He agreed that the assassination had to be carried out, but he would help out with a few dollars only if she would tell the whole group about it.

Something doesn't make sense. If Emma had come to Most and told him the whole story, he would have advised against it; but if he agreed, wouldn't he have given her the money?

She writes that she had to ride back and forth on the El[56] the whole night because her friends wouldn't let her in when her landlord wanted to evict her. Emma's friends would certainly have let her in to spend the night; they wouldn't close the door and then get their housekeeper to tell her that she couldn't stay. If they didn't want her to stay longer, her friends would have told her in the morning. And where was her friend Fedya? He had his own room. Couldn't she stay a night with him? And where were all her good friends? Most had sinned so terribly against her that she found it necessary to strike him with a horsewhip and take revenge on him?[57] Did Emma Goldman consider herself better or more important than the movement for which she was always ready to sacrifice and give her life? Listen: she bought a horsewhip and took two of her bodyguards with her to that meeting. Her companions carried iron rods under their coats. (Emma doesn't say anything in her book about iron, but I know about it because I was there.) When Most started to speak she came up to him and begin to lash at him with her horsewhip. Can't she understand that the shame that night was her own and not Most's? She surely knew that Most, a gentleman, would not hit her back because she was a woman.

Yes, this is certainly striking evidence of what a heroine she was and how she sacrificed herself for the cause. When Emma prepared for her heroic deed with the whip, did she think about the impact this would have on the movement, on her ideal? No, she thought only about one thing—about the great, heroic Emma Goldman. It wouldn't have bothered her if she and Most had come to blows, because her two bodyguards would have used their iron rods to protect her. She didn't give that a thought. The movement wasn't in her mind at that moment.

I write these things now and recall these sad facts only because this question is drilled into my brain: Emma committed heroic deeds in her youth—did she want no one to remember them anymore, and to bury them in the past? So Emma comes and writes about it [the horsewhip incident] with such generosity and with such triumph, like a heroic deed. Is that right? Emma had always preached that the man who worked on behalf of the movement must always subordinate his own interests for the benefit of the movement. But Emma did the exact opposite: she trampled on the movement with her feet, to advance her own interests. How did people expect to win new recruits for the ideal, for the movement, with such a scandal out in the open? I think that the horse-whip with which she struck Most, also struck her. And one more thing: how is it that, after the scandal with the whip, Emma made several attempts to become good friends with

Most again? It's inconceivable to me that, on the one hand, you can sell yourself on the street for the movement—for your ideal—and on the other hand give such moral blows?

A Horrible Night—A Struggle With a Human Beast

A night that I will never forget. My sister Rochel and I were walking home from work, or rather, sliding home. A cold winter rain had come down all day, and by nightfall, it was even colder and the rain had turned into a damp snow. It was wet and slippery. The path from the factory where we worked was long and had a lot of little holes, filled with half-frozen water.

My sister said, "You know, Helene, I've never fallen during the winter," and as soon as she said those words, she was lying in one of the holes. While trying to drag her out, I also fell in. We didn't stop falling until we got home—first my sister, then me; or first me, then my sister.

When we got up to our room, we were both so wet through and through that pools of water streamed from our clothing and our shoes squeaked. We immediately turned on the stove, which we had prepared in the morning so that we only needed to light a match. A fire quickly began to burn and the little room warmed up pleasantly. We took of our wet things, pulled down our socks, and put on old house-clothes and shoes. We hung our things on ropes next to the stove so they would dry. We made some tea to warm our numb bones.

When the tea was ready, Rochel laid out two cups. We felt as if we were sitting in a [parlor?]. I took the cup of tea in both hands and held it to my lips. All of a sudden, there was a knock at the door and in walked a girl we knew (we had eaten supper at her parents' home). She held a telegram, which she gave to me. I put down the tea and read it. Frightened, I jumped up and handed it to my sister. It was a message from my brother-in-law in New Haven, where he and my sister Anna were living. He said that Anna had again become very ill, and he insisted that I come and help him save her. My heart was torn with the dreaded thought that my sister was again in danger. This time the misfortune was even greater than before, when we tore her from the Angel of Death's hands. Now she had a three-month-old baby and her good, loyal husband would not be able to endure this misfortune.

73

My sister and I looked over the telegram in silence with shocked expressions. There was no doubt that I had to go to them, but we had no money for the trip, and I didn't own a pair of dry socks. I started to put on my wet socks and dress. My friend had gone home and returned with a few dollars for my journey. I left the cup of tea and the warmth of our little room.

Previously when I went to New Haven, I would take the boat that left at midnight and I'd arrive around five or six o'clock in the morning. I went by boat because it was cheaper. In our circumstances, we only did what was cheaper. But this time I didn't consider the cheapest option, because I wanted to get to my sister as quickly as possible. By train I could arrive three or four hours earlier than the boat—at around two o'clock in the morning. I was certain that this is what my brother-in-law expected me to do and that he'd meet me at the train.

I really didn't want to leave the warm room and it pained me to leave my little sister all alone in her frightened state, but I couldn't help it. My sister gave me an umbrella, which I, in my flustered state, hadn't thought of, and I left quickly for New York, where I took the train to New Haven. Fortunately, I got there at the right time, running, with my cold, wet clothes and my dark thoughts. I pushed and pushed so the train would bring me even faster to my ailing sister. I thought about my two sisters: the younger, alas, alone in the deserted attic room in Newark and the other, the ailing one, the young mother who once again was wrestling with death.

The train arrived in New Haven at around two o'clock in the morning, and I was positive that my brother-in-law would be waiting for me. However, when I got off the train, I didn't see him; I searched everywhere—no brother-in-law! I was alone. All the passengers had already left the station—some went by themselves, others were picked up. I stood all alone in the deep snow, trembling from the cold in my wet clothes. It was terribly cold. The snow was coming down heavily, and it was very slippery. I set off on my way, sliding more than walking. I wandered back and forth because I didn't know the way from the train to my sister's. I only knew the way from the boat. I walked, and every so often I'd slip. I looked around to see if I recognized any of the streets leading to my sister's house.

A policeman, who apparently had an eye on me, shouted after me, "Hey, sister, where are you from and where are you going? Now is not the time for a young woman to be wandering the streets." I went up to him and in tears told him everything. I gave him my sister's address, begging him to help me get there. He said that he couldn't leave his "beat," but he would find someone who could bring me to my sister's.

We walked for a while, then a young man turned up. The policeman called him over and asked him if he knew the way I needed to go.

"Yes, officer," said the young man. He said that he was going that very way and would bring me to my sister's. On the way, the young man was very polite and friendly to me; he wanted to carry my umbrella, like a gentleman, but I wouldn't give it to him. Somehow I feared that he wouldn't give it back to me.

We continued to walk. The streets were very unfamiliar to me, even though I knew New Haven from before. The journey somehow seemed too long. The young man started to move closer to me. I was slipping the whole time and he caught me and held me up. Suddenly he started to grab me. I tore myself away from him and began to run. I fell and he grabbed me back. It was very dark, and only the snow illuminated the path. It was dead quiet all around; not a living soul was to be seen. Suddenly my companion caught me and dragged me into a narrow side street, a tiny dark alley. I couldn't see anything. I only heard and felt the heavy breathing of the angry, two-footed animal next to me. Soon I would faint out of fear, but the idea came to me that I wasn't allowed to be weak right now. On the contrary, I had to strengthen myself; I had to defend myself. I became desperate. How could I defend myself against this terrible danger? I felt the umbrella in my hand, and it seemed like a living thing, a friend in my time of need. I began to lash out with the umbrella right and left. I struck all around and with all my might, more than my usual strength would have allowed me. And I hit my mark. I repelled every attack from this human animal. On a cold, slippery, dark winter night, a weak and distressed girl battled with a human beast. The battle-arena was a narrow one. I hit my mark. I hit it. I was certain that I hit it because the scoundrel had cried out in pain a few times. He couldn't avoid my blows with the umbrella. I felt as if I were a wild, provoked animal, struggling in the jungle against animals wilder and larger than she.

Eventually I felt that I was free, that no one was fighting with me anymore. I didn't know, however, if he had run away or had fallen down, or if I had killed him. I knew and felt only one thing—I was free! The air was pure. I no longer felt or heard the hot and heavy breath from this angry and wild human beast. I began to walk down the narrow alley. The umbrella was in pieces, so I threw it away. I had lost my hat, and my head ached due to the hair-pulling. My clothes were torn. My face was bloody. Flailing wildly with the umbrella, I had also given myself a few strong blows. But I felt good. I was over-joyed. I walked and walked and fell, and walked some more. At first, the streets were unfamiliar to me and I was afraid even to look for a policeman who could give me directions. Walking thus, wildly and at random, I finally saw some familiar streets that led to my sister's place. I now walked with certainty, completely free. I knew where I was.

When I arrived at my sister's house, I recalled why I had come in the first place and my hands and feet began to tremble. Perhaps it was already too late. I bent down to the keyhole and listened with a wild-ly beating heart in the night silence. I thought someone was crying. The cry was so quiet and so sad.... A shiver shook through me. It's no use.... It's no use. Too late! Oh, my poor sister! My poor brother-in-law! Her dear, good comrade! And the poor child is, alas, an orphan. Oh, what shall I do for them? How can I help them?

Silent and with intense fear, I knocked on the door. Quietly I called, "Sam, where are you? Open the door! Let me in." I heard my sister's voice, "Sam, Sam, someone is knocking on the door. Go open up!" The door opened. I fell right into by brother-in-law's arms.

"My sister lives, she lives!" I ran through. Nothing else mattered now.

When I calmed down, my brother-in-law explained that he ex-pected me to arrive by boat in the morning, which is why he didn't meet me at the train. He said that my sister had become ill, and the doctor had forbidden her from nursing the child. She had contracted milk fever and it would be better for the baby to take a bottle. In her fever, Anna was constantly calling out "Helene!" and asking that I be brought to her at once. She said that she was dying and she wanted to give me her child. That's why she had Sam send the telegram.

I stayed as needed with my sister and her son. I didn't have a clue how to take care of a child or prepare the bottles, however, I managed the job properly. Oh, how lovely and sweet the baby was to me! When I took his soft, warm body in my arms, my soul went out to him.

I stayed there for two weeks until the baby got used to the bottle and didn't cry as much, and by then my sister was out of her fever and back to normal. I did what I could until my father came from New York to take my place. It was no longer so difficult to care for them. My sister was already a lot better.

Now—a joke. The day after I arrived in New Haven, I became terribly tired and worn out in the evening because of my experiences the previous night. My sister was busy with some guests, so I threw myself down on the sofa and immediately fell fast asleep. Seeing that I was lying on the hard sofa, my brother-in-law brought a pillow. He slowly raised my head and put the pillow underneath. I jumped up and started hitting with both fists shouting and abusing him. In my dream I had been striking my companion, the bum, with the umbrella. And I also thought that I was joking with Most, so I shouted: "Let me rest! I don't want to speak with you!" The last words I said in German.

"*Jawohl*," my brother-in-law answered in German. "She lets me place the pillow under her head!" I woke up and we all laughed.

I arrived back in New York on a Sunday. Before I went to my sister, I had gone to the Sunday meeting where Most spoke. This was the historical meeting about which I wrote in the previous chapter. This night, Emma Goldman showed her heroism by attacking Most and lashing out at him with a horse-whip in her hand. Seeing this, I fainted.

I Become the *Freiheit*'s Bookkeeper[58]

Time went on. One day Most suggested that I quit my job in the factory and start working for his weekly newspaper, *Freiheit*. He taught me the simple bookkeeping that the newspaper used. I'd become so exhausted from my work at that factory that I was unable to stand on my two feet; it was difficult for me to attend meetings, and, most important, to do things for the movement.

"Since you already understand enough German and can manage the correspondence, send bills, and do some simple bookkeeping, you can work at the *Freiheit*," Most told me. "The work will be more interesting for you, it will strain you less, and you'll be closer to the movement. I will match what you earn in the shop. You will have more time to develop yourself and to read." It was a very logical suggestion, yet it took me a while to accept it. I was afraid. I thought that the other comrades would misinterpret it.

Around that time, I became sick at work, so I eventually decided to accept Most's suggestion and began working in the *Freiheit* editorial office. I rented a room from a very cooperative family with whom I had become acquainted in Newark. Most came to see me every night, except when we went to meetings. Thus gradually it happened that Most and I came together as man and wife.

At the time, Most was already very tired from the great, bitter struggle that he was leading by himself. The men with whom he had established the *Freiheit* had begun to argue with him due to the fact that he didn't allow them to dictate what and how he wrote in the paper. Most wanted to run the paper his way, so they considered him a despot, a boss. Being connected to the *Freiheit*, I had an opportunity to witness the struggle, but also Most as a combatant.

Most's Life Up Until I Became Acquainted With Him

I will now offer a short overview of Johann Most's life up until the time I became acquainted with him. Most was born to very poor but very intelligent parents. His father, Josef Most, worked for a lawyer for very little money. His salary was so small that when he first met his future wife, Most's mother, who was a governess, he wasn't able to marry her.[59] At that time in Germany there was a law that a man had to earn a certain amount of money to be able to marry—Josef Most didn't even earn that amount. But love knows no impediment or shackles, and with his parents' help, they were able to arrange things without an official wedding. And so, his beloved came to live in the house as their housemaid. Johann Most thus came into the world as an illegitimate child, "to spite the police," as he used to say in his humorous manner.[60]

When Most was two-and-half years old, his father's circumstances improved, and his parents were able to legally marry. Most described his parent's romance very realistically and humorously. Even now, the picture is right before my eyes: I can clearly see the poor little house;

his parents, dressed in their Sunday clothes, are in a festive mood. Outside stands the little wagon that would carry the pair to the church. They marry legally. Next to the happy couple stands a little boy with long golden hair, dressed in a velvet suit that his mother had made for him, and a white shirt with a big pointed collar. His big blue eyes gaze with wonder at his parents. His pale, delicate face reveals a childlike curiosity. He watches as if something extraordinary is about to happen, although he doesn't understand what. He wants to travel with his parents to the church, but they, naturally, can't bring him. They climb into the wagon. The old couple looks out the window. The neighbors are also looking at the young couple going to their wedding. Little Johann takes advantage of the opportunity when his grandparents are looking out the window, and runs out to the wagon, crying that his parents should bring him to the church.

"I want to be at your wedding," cried the little Johann. The neighbors break out into laughter and his grandmother runs out of the house and takes him back inside. She runs with burning cheeks because of the neighbors' insulting laughter. Although great poverty ruled the home, Most enjoyed a happy childhood. His parents showered him with love and tenderness since, because of their poverty, they couldn't give him anything else.

When he was seven, something happened that caused Most misfortune for the rest of his life: he caught a head cold.[61] His palate became swollen and began to rot. His parents did everything possible to help their child but, alas, could not accomplish anything. Medical science at the time was quite poor, and the doctors couldn't find a remedy. The illness crawled along like a snake, gradually consuming his bones. It made him weak. Years went by and the unfortunate child suffered from terrible pain.

When Most was ten years old, he met with a new misfortune: cholera broke out in Augsburg, Bayern, where Most lived with his parents. During the epidemic, almost all of the Most family perished: grandparents, mother, and several children.[62] Only his father, sister, and he, the ailing Johann (or Hans, as his parents used to call him) remained. When his beloved mother was torn from him, he felt as if the earth under his weak legs began to crumble. It took him quite a while to find his balance. Oh, how he missed his good, intelligent, loving mother! The illness had sapped his zest for life. His jawbone continued to rot and the poor child suffered great pain. His father didn't know what to do. He couldn't attend to his two orphans because he had to go to the office every day and didn't have anyone to run the house for him.

Eventually he decided to marry again and so he did. The woman he married was very different from his first wife.[63] She was—as Most tells it—a cast-off. She was very pious, mean, and stingy. She was also jealous of the two poor children and their mother's memory, which their father honored. His father was busy in the office all day, and in the evening had to give lessons to support his family, which had quickly increased in numbers. So the two poor children were left at the mercy (or lack of mercy) of the evil stepmother. She hated the children, and they felt her hate with her full hand. She treated them like servants and made them take care of her children. Johann had to wash diapers, rock and nurse the babies, go shopping, and chop wood. He used to receive blows for every little thing that he did incorrectly, or when he'd take care of his little sister, Paula.[64]

The children were often hungry because the poverty was severe and it was difficult to fill so many mouths. Of course, his stepmother filled the mouths of her own children. Often little Johann had to steal something from the grocery for him and his sister to eat, and if he got caught he'd receive a good smack. It became unbearable for the poor boy. His stepmother would report him to his father. Most's father was exhausted from working hard all day and didn't have the patience to verify the complaints, so he would beat the ailing boy. After this punishment, little Johann would run away from home and sleep in a vacant field somewhere.

It also happened that his father would become upset at his wife, recognizing that he was being unfair to his children because of her. Then he'd become so wild that he would be ready to murder her; he'd grab her by the throat and choke her until she turned blue. In these conditions, love could find no place in young Johann's heart. On the contrary, his heart was filled with hate and bitterness.

A famous surgeon arrived in town,[65] when he was fourteen and his illness had sapped his blood and health, so Most's father decided to bring the unfortunate Johann to this important doctor. After the great professor had examined the boy, he declared that the illness had reached its final stage and the only recourse was an extremely dangerous operation. On the other hand, if they didn't operate, the boy would have no chance to live because the jawbone was already decaying, and at most he would live another year. If he were to get the operation, he could die under the knife or he could recover. His father decided to go with the operation.

While the surgery was being planned, the sickly boy heard his stepmother say to her neighbor, "Oh, I hope I will finally be rid of him and he won't return from the operation." Little Johann went up to this wicked woman, his stepmother, looked her in the face with hatred, and said that he would come back just to spite her.

And he kept his word—he returned. The operation was successful. Yes, his life was saved, but a terrible effect remained. His face was horribly misshapen—a caricature of a person. The jawbone on one side of his face was completely removed. The sick side appeared to be without a cheek, and the healthy side was swollen. He remained this way his entire life.[66] It's therefore no surprise that further bitterness and hatred accumulated in Most's injured heart.

His physical suffering and his spiritual troubles—together they made him what he was: a bitter, disappointed, and unhappy boy.

And yet something great and strong developed in him that made him want to live and conquer the entire world. Because of the trials he endured in his earliest years, he hated those who had all the pleasure in life, who had everything without working for it themselves, those who ruled the world. He began to hate the powerful, those who had everything yet abused the helpless poor and enslaved the masses. It irked him that those who had everything and were in a position to help the wretched, didn't do so. He couldn't be indifferent to the injustice that appeared before his eyes. He wasn't religious and didn't believe that God had thus arranged this world. Even in school he couldn't witness the inequality, unfairness, and harshness of the teachers, and he often rebelled. He influenced other students to rebel, and once they held a strike, which Most led. It was a protest against the teachers' harsh disciplinary manner.

Johann Most's First Strike

Most organized his first protest against society when he was still a boy: a student strike in his school. The strike concluded with Most being expelled. With that, his education ended.[67] His father was wild with anger at his son the rebel. He told him that he had to learn a trade, that he would no longer support him. Most was a little over fourteen at the time.

He chose to learn bookbinding, and didn't know himself why he'd chosen to pursue that trade in particular. His father didn't care what his son learned. He was happy that it would bring an end to the ongoing arguments about the boy between him and his wife, and it would be one less mouth to fill. His father took Johann to a master-bookbinder, and left him there to learn the trade.[68] In those days it was customary that a boy wanting to learn a profession had to sign a three-year contract with a master craftsman; he would live with the master and bring with him his own bed and bedding, pay for having clothes laundered, etc. Work-hours were from dawn until late at night. An apprentice didn't receive any money, only board. He slept in the attic. An apprentice had to do a lot of work around the house. He had to do all kinds of errands: watch the children, clean everyone's shoes, wash the dishes, and many other tasks. When he completed this work after three years, he had learned the trade and become a journeyman; he was free to venture into the world on his own two feet.

This is what young Johann Most went through. He endured all kinds of experiences, insults and bitterness, and didn't lack in beatings. He was beaten all the more, because he would never give up without a fight. He also suffered due to his disfigured face; he was called all kinds of names, and children on the street would follow him. He was small in stature, skinny, and pale. All this together had, unfortunately, embittered him. He was excitable, hot-tempered, and angry. He would often respond to his master with a sharp tongue and would therefore receive blows from him and also from his father, when the master would report on him. He endured all of this and learned the skills well. The books that were delivered to be repaired were often interesting for the apprentice, and at night he would take them up to his room in the attic and study them until late. If he hadn't finished the book, he'd bring it back in the morning and hide it so no one could find it, and then at night he would take it again. One time, the entire house was turned upside-down in the search for a book. When it was found, poor Johann received many blows. Yes, the master and his apprentice didn't like each other much.

Most had a great passion for the theater. Obviously, he was unable to go to the theater the regular way because he never had money to buy a ticket, so he found a way to sneak in. His master didn't want him going, and sternly forbid it. So Most would sneak out of the house and afterwards sneak back in, and he would get a good beating if the master caught him. However, this didn't stop him from going. Most would often get caught in the theater itself and would be beaten and thrown out. In his heart he felt an intense longing to act. He had a burning desire to express on stage the feelings that had accumulated inside him through his unhappy life. He didn't see any way to realize his fervent wish because of his disfigured face.

Finally, Most had fulfilled his contract and was free to enter the world. The future seemed very uncertain to him. The many blows he received gave him a lot of experience in his young life. From the books with torn covers that he'd read, he accumulated knowledge and philosophical views on life. With a great sigh, mixed with the joy that he was now free, he packed up his few old things, said goodbye to his master, and went out in the wide world. The sky was gray, the world big and wide. Life spread out before him. Although he loved his father, Most harbored a lot of resentment in his heart for all the suffering that he'd endured from his stepmother. He said a cold goodbye to his father.[69]

Thus began a life of wandering his native country, as well as others. He traveled for about five years, mostly walking because he didn't have the money to travel by train or coach. He visited many great cities and towns. He sought work, but it was difficult to find any because he was very small and thin, and his crippled face and shabby clothes didn't make a good impression. It was mainly his face that hindered him getting work. He was sent from one place to another. In one place he was told he was too small, too weak, and that he would not be capable of producing enough work. Another told him that he was too ugly, that the prospective employer's wife was pregnant and could not stand to look at him. Yet another told him that the customers would be afraid if they saw him and would run away. And when he would get upset from this fine how-do-you-do, and would say something back, they would threaten to summon the police if he didn't go quickly. And so it went. He became very depressed and began to contemplate suicide. But soon he reassured himself; his youth and his will to live, to study the world, helped him to overcome those feelings. Sometimes he succeeded in getting a little work. The work was very difficult, the hours long, the pay very little, the food bad and insufficient, and the master craftsmen mean and harsh. This is how he muddled through.

Most Begins His Wandering

Most was able to support himself through the winter months, but when spring came, he started to feel wanderlust. As it happened, he and his current master had quarreled, so he quit his job and ventured on his way to wander.

The poor, beleaguered little rebel set out on his wanderings without the labor movement. His youthful spirit quickly recognized, his eyes quickly saw, and his heart was quickly aroused. His inborn intelligence and his broad understanding helped him understand the world. His embittered and grieving heart was drawn to struggle; his hatred began to grow. Most discovered the workers' meetings and organizations everywhere he went. He began to study the whole question of the worker and the worker's movement, and to participate in discussions. He was immediately accepted into the movement and soon was welcomed at all the meetings. It was during this time of wandering that he really found himself. He would beg for a little bread at the big summer hotels, and he would stop at all the hotels, big and small, and ask the owners if they would let him recite or sing something (he had a fine, soft, pleasant voice). He was usually a big hit with the guests, and they would give him food and some money. He would typically sleep in a vacant field. With the money he received from the guests, he bought a shirt, a pair of socks, a pair of old pants, some cheap shoes and such things, and when winter arrived he looked for work. When he found it, he would stay at his job until the spring.

He began to take a much stronger role in the labor movement. He gave speeches and wrote articles for different newspapers.

One time he found work with a nice, decent master who treated him very well, and they became friends, but unfortunately this good luck didn't last long. Times were bad and the master didn't have enough work and had to let him go. They parted as good friends; a warm spot for this friendly man always remained in Most's heart.[70] Such was Most's wandering.

Young Most Starts to be Heard

Soon Most's voice was heard both near and far, and his pen became recognizable. His spirit grew. He was banished from some cities as a dangerous agitator, and it wasn't long before Most began wandering again, this time from one prison to another. He roamed the entire county and spent time in different prisons, using the time to read books and study the history of the labor movement. He couldn't make a living from his skills anymore, partially because he didn't have any time, but also because his name was recognized everywhere and no one wanted to hire a dangerous agitator.

At last, Most threw himself body and soul into the movement; he helped establish newspapers and organize unions. He wasn't compensated for this work, because most of these projects lacked money and so he often went hungry, sleeping in the offices of these penniless newspapers. From time to time he would earn a little money so that he could preserve his soul and cover his body. When he got older Most grew a beard, which enabled him to hide his disfigured face. He was somewhat liberated from his bitter feelings.

Eventually Most became an outspoken Social Democrat, and labored with his entire passionate nature. He penned pamphlets and took part in every venture in the service of his ideal. Once, at a time of reactionary persecutions by the government against socialists, free-speech, and the right to assemble, the workers decided to plan a huge demonstration. The demonstrators marched to parliament, and Most marched in line. The workers desired freedom of speech and assembly. Some of them—the ringleaders—were arrested. Most found himself arrested, charged with treason, and sentenced to four years in prison.[71] Most's father came to help him, and sent petitions to the highest judges until he succeeded in getting a promise that his son would be pardoned if he signed his name to a plea for mercy. Most's father wrote to him and pleaded with him to do it, and noted that, as his father, he had a right to demand that he do it. Most answered his father with a letter full of indignation:

"What? I will plead for forgiveness, for mercy when I was the one who suffered and was insulted? The judgment against me was unfair. No! I will never do this. I will never buy my freedom through humiliation and thus forever besmirch my name and my ideal!"

His father argued and begged him to recognize his error, declare himself guilty, and ask for a pardon. But Most rejected his father with great indignation. Later, in a long letter, Most explained to his father why he hadn't agreed with him. That letter was then used against him in court.[72] Among other things he wrote:

> I have not concealed my principles from You (Most used the formal tense with his father) and You cannot prevent me from having them, and I see no reason why I should feel or act like a lost son just because I have not replaced my republican convictions for your monarchist ones. You may think to yourself that I can buy my freedom and my happiness, but I want to tell You that there could be no greater tragedy for me than to be compelled to act against my own beliefs. For the greatest prize I wouldn't do it. You must realize that it is always better and more honest when a person acts according to his own convictions rather than to change his colors with the weather or with circumstances.
>
> I could have played the role of hypocrite and liar and told You all kinds of sweet things and phrases that You wished to hear, instead of letting my pen tell You the truth. But how could You expect me to do that? Did You really think that I would speak differently to my father than to the rest of the world? Did You really think that I would not say to You what I preach to the masses? I can assure You that while You suggest to me a life of luxury and wealth, that I should act against my principles and my comrades, I would rather choose a life of starvation, suffering, and poverty. I would not think for a minute about how to respond to your suggestion.[73]

Most sat in jail for a long time. A change in government then brought amnesty to all political prisoners. Soon after, Most became the greatest agitator of his time. He traveled to different cities in Germany, Austria, Italy, and Hungary, and awakened the enslaved working masses to fight against their oppressors.[74] And he paid for this with prison. When he was free, he would often be expelled from the cities he visited for being a dangerous agitator.[75]

Most Gets Married

In time, Most became acquainted with a girl and married her. However, he didn't know how to lead a normal family life, due to his activities in the movement. He had children, but he couldn't experience fatherly joy. He couldn't live a separate private life; his life belonged to the masses, to whom he had already long devoted himself, and whom he served with his whole, vast soul. He barely saw his children. They were born when he was in prison, and they died when he was again in jail.[76]

At one point he was arrested and put in prison for twenty-six months, leaving his wife alone; she couldn't bear it any more and left him. Shortly after that she died of illness.[77] Oh, how many wounds this unfortunate death caused to his heart!

Most Goes to England

Most began to distance himself from his Social Democratic friends and began to study anarchism. He became more radical, and as a result, of course, his comrades, the Social Democrats, turned against him. Most traveled to England.

Most went on his way alone. In London, he established the *Freiheit*. He continued to starve, to wear old clothes, and to sleep in an office. Studying anarchism, Most became convinced that it was the closest and best path to the liberation of humanity, so he gave himself over entirely to this idea.

He found, however, that he stood alone in his new convictions. His comrades, the Social Democrats, refused to help him. They didn't want to help him publish the anarchist *Freiheit*. He remained alone in his struggle, with the exception of one loyal friend and comrade whom he had brought with him and who remained by his side.[78] Most spent a number of years in England, leading the battle and enlightening the masses. He was often sent to prison.[79]

Most greeted the assassination of Alexander II with great enthusiasm in *Freiheit* and for that he was imprisoned. After his release, Most could no longer find work in London. As he sat in prison, his printing shop was ruined, so he had to seek another location for his activities. And he chose—America.[80]

Most Comes to America

Most came to America alone, without a wife or children. Here, in this free country, he began a new chapter in his life. He quickly made friends and created a new domain for his work. He began to publish *Freiheit* and spearheaded anarchist propaganda. Here he starved anew. He slept in the editorial office on a cavernous sofa.[81]

The movement went up and down. Great enthusiasm would immediately be followed by harsh reaction. When I came here as a little girl, I still heard the outcry over the terrible tragedy that had played out a short time before in Chicago.[82] The air still echoed with the speeches that the accused gave in court at the trial. This tragedy had stunned people of all classes, as well as the labor movement. It initiated the harassment of and incitements against workers. The glowing movement was left in ashes—but the ashes only covered the fire; they didn't extinguish it. The police, those capitalist servants, very much wanted to bring Most to Chicago, and sought to drag him into the Chicago trial. If they had succeeded, the movement would have lost him, and I would never have met him.[83]

Most threw himself into the movement with fresh courage. His work was now bound up with many more risks and challenges than previously. It was up to him to revive the flame that had been snuffed by the heap of ashes.

My Feelings For Most[******]

I have never before given an account of my feelings for Most. Naturally, I was not in love with him like a young woman loves the man whom she marries. This was impossible. He was very dear to me. For me, he was the symbol of greater, more significant, and holier work. He played a huge role in my life. An inner force drew me to him so that I would hold this symbol dear, take care of him, give him a new life and new power, and not permit him to suffer. The movement, which became my life's work, was closely tied with Most. I accepted my feelings for him as love.

A huge storm broke out when Most and I got together. Each person interpreted our relationship his own way, that is, according to how that individual looked at life in general and on our ideal in particular. Some said that I had done it because of Most's name. But

[******]Minkin resumes her main narrative.

what could Most's name have been for me? This name, which Most had made for himself through a life of suffering, struggle, and inexhaustible labor, was his own. I didn't have anything to do with it. He was already famous when I became acquainted with him. A person has to make his own name. It's true, one can in private, behind walls and closed doors, make sacrifices and create more than those who walk around in public making names for themselves. But the names of these silent creators and martyrs rarely come out into the light of the world. I know that I have quietly served my ideal, suffered, and endured great sacrifices by helping Most bear his heavy burden, by making him a little happy, by helping him through some tough times and bitter disappointments. Every time Most tired from the grueling battle and wanted to lay down his weapons, I wouldn't let him. I gave him fresh courage to live and fight again.

It was a difficult and bitter struggle for me but I endured. Of one thing I am certain: No one can say that I was with Most for his money or for his nice, comfortable life. Everyone in the movement knew that we lived in the severest poverty.

Our First Apartment

Our first place was in Brooklyn, in a basement.[84] We paid six dollars a month in rent. The apartment consisted of three "rooms." In reality, it was one big room divided with walls to create two additional rooms—two boxes, lacking windows, light, air, and any comfort. I made one of the boxes into a bedroom. I'd brought my old furniture from my attic-space in Newark: a bed, a chair, and a couple of hooks for the wall on which to hang clothes—this was the only furniture in the bedroom.

The "parlor," or front room, had two windows that looked directly out onto the sidewalk. In the room stood an old divan that Most had brought from his office, my round table, a bureau, and a few chairs. I made the other "box" into the kitchen. I bought a large box at a dry-goods store, which served as a table. Inside the box I placed some hooks on which I hung the pots. In one corner, another small box held the dishes: plates, cups, saucers, spoons, forks, knives, etc. An additional little box served as a chair. In the other corner was a wooden washtub. I covered everything with unbleached muslin so it wouldn't look so unappealing. In both the bedroom and the "parlor," I also covered everything with unbleached muslin, which I had trimmed with cotton of different colors. Curtains hung on the two low windows. All the walls of the "parlor" were hung with pictures. We had pictures of the Chicago martyrs. Most had gathered all kinds of pictures from the movement, which he attached to a large board wreathed with a frame of red fabric that we used to use at different events. Some of the images, which depicted scenes from past moments in labor history, such as the battle of the Paris Commune, I framed in purple mixed with black fabric. I made a bookshelf out of a box where I put all my books and many of Most's. Altogether our house made an imaginative, artistic impression. The room (the "parlor") was filled with interesting recollections of labor history. Each image spoke to me and told me about the ever-bitter struggle of our movement. Looking at the image of the Paris Commune, I saw how Louise Michel stood on the battlefield with a rifle in her hand and fought for the suffering masses.[85] I felt as if I had also taken part in all these historical struggles.

I stopped working in the *Freiheit* office because I was expecting a child, but I continued to look after the bookkeeping. Most brought me the books, as well as each day's letters and I managed everything from home.

The Comrades Persecute Most For Having a Family Life

Alas, the comrades didn't treat us very well—not as you might expect comrades to do. They harassed Most—for taking the liberty of starting a family. A young wife, a child, and perhaps more children! That's not for Most—they complained. That's not for a revolutionary. A fighter must give up his life to the world, the ideal. But they themselves, these very comrades, all had families and enjoyed the warmth of family life. But they refused Most the very same right.

Most would say to me, "They think (the comrades that persecuted and rebuked him) that the blood in my veins flows only for shouting, speaking; they think, that my heart beats only for the movement; they think that my brains work only for creating, writing, and agitating, and as soon as I fulfill my duty toward the movement, my hot blood turns to cold water; my brains wither and I float in the air until the next opportunity when I must again agitate, shout, speak, write, go to prison, and so on."

Yes, these comrades considered it a terrible misfortune for the movement that Most had started a family; and they did everything they could to disrupt his family life. They whispered in his ear all kinds of "secrets", rumors, and gossip. They raised doubts and mistrust of me in his heart, and because I am by nature a sensitive, withdrawn person, this caused me great pain. In my very heart, it struck me as if they had stuck sharp spears in my heart and it sprung holes. It also pained me that they took away my faith in them, my belief in humanity, in brotherhood, in friendship—the friendship that I had always demonstrated to them. Slowly I built myself an inner life and withdrew from the comrades. Now I lived for Most, and for the child that I was expecting.

I Become a Mother

I would dream about my child: what will I do for my child? How will I raise her, if it's a girl? I didn't want a daughter because I knew the life of a woman. In the current order, a woman is [segregated?] from a man. She is often compelled to live in the narrow confines of her four walls, while caring for the house and the children. The woman must retreat from normal life while the man remains in the realm of [society?].

A huge change was coming to our lives: Most was going to be a father. His life went along as usual, but I stayed at home. Most was thrilled with the pregnancy. He had already had three children[86] in his younger years, and he never expected that he would again be a father. His past experience brought him terrible pain. Unfortunately, he was never able to rejoice with his children since he hadn't been able to see them. Maybe it's true that a man who dedicates his whole life to the movement should not have a family.

I remained at home. Over the course of time, shadows began to sneak into my house. Something unexpected, unconscious had struck fear in my heart; I felt like a child left alone in the dark and was afraid when I heard or thought that something was creeping around in the house. Shortly before our first child was born, Most would often speak with me about his younger days. His children with his first wife came into the world and left it before he was able to experience the joy of being a father to them. They were born when he was in prison and they died when he was also behind bars. Tears would run down his face when he spoke of them, and I would cry along with him. My heart trembled for my child every time I felt his weak movements inside. I was afraid without knowing why.

I tried to chase the dark thoughts away. I wanted to be happy, to laugh, sing and to hope for the best. I would say to myself that I would be a mother and a father to my son. I didn't want to drag Most away from his activities for even a minute. I hoped that when Most had a child, a boy (I don't know why but I was certain that I was expecting a son), his love for his son would lend him more courage for his struggles. It would bring him a little personal happiness. It would make everything in his life more interesting. When he would come home and take his child in his arms—it would give him a zest for life.

The cellar where we were living was damp and I began to feel uneasy. I was afraid for the child. It would not be a healthy place for him, and while materially it was difficult for us to pay more rent, we decided to move out of the cellar to a healthier place. It was also too far for Most to come home for lunch, and I wanted him to be able to come home to eat, take a little nap, and see his child every day.

We took a top floor apartment on Henry Street in New York. The rent was eleven dollars a month. We felt that we were living very extravagantly but we couldn't find anything cheaper. I arranged our new place so that the better room—the living room, a front room with two big windows—would be the bedroom, so when the child came, he would have enough fresh air. The bed, the bureau, and a few chairs stood in the bedroom. The smaller bedroom I made into a writing room for Most. There was a sofa, the bookshelf, and a little table covered with an oil-cloth, which served as a desk. I hung the pictures on the room's walls and it really looked very interesting and pleasant. The kitchen was our living room—kitchen and dining room together.

That was in 1894. On the 19th of May, our first child was born. The delivery was difficult because I was undernourished; I didn't have the strength to give nature a hand. The child was also too weak to help in the process, and he probably had no great longing to come into a world as beautiful as this. I'll never forget how Most looked that day. After so many years, I cry while writing these lines just as he cried then and as I myself cried watching him. While I was wrangling with death, Most had come to me and given me his head. I, not knowing what was going on, tore his hair with my last bit of strength while he stroked me, caressed me, cried intensely, and at the same time laughed hysterically.

A little later—when the child had come into this world—my sister Anna arrived from Boston. Most ran up to her with indescribable joy, his eyes burning like torches and his face aflame. He was burning up as if in fever. He embraced my sister and kissed her joyfully.

"Sister-in-law, sister-in-law, we have a son! We have a new soldier for our cause!" he shouted.

We were very poor and the child needed to have good care. My sister Rochel loaned us a few dollars for an inexpensive carriage for him, and I paid the debt back fifty cents a week. The carriage was kept in the cellar and every day when I wanted to give the child some fresh air, I had to endure a great struggle: with the child in one hand, and the pillows, the bottle, and other things in the other hand, I would go down the four flights. There I would ask my neighbor if she would hold the baby while I went to the cellar to bring up the carriage. Coming back was the same. Many days I sat with the child on the roof because it was too difficult for me to get the carriage. When Most traveled on a protest trip around the country for three months, I was left alone with the ailing child and often without the money to buy him milk.[87] But I always found ways to get milk for my baby.

I decided that I would not have any more children because it was impossible to live under these conditions. But when I made that decision, I didn't know that a second son was already on the way.[88] I was too young and inexperienced in life. Most was overjoyed with his two beautiful sons, but joy was all he offered them and me; poverty bore down on us even more now.

I didn't hinder Most in his activities. On the contrary, I helped as much as possible. All the challenges of raising two children without money so that they, the children, should not suffer—these I took on all by myself so that none of his comrades could remain aloof and accuse him of giving his time and energy to his family rather than to the movement. In reality, it was often like this: he would come home exhausted, shattered from the grueling struggle within the movement, from many bitter disappointments, and would throw himself down to sleep after spending some leisure time with his family.

Often when he had to speak at a meeting in the evening, he would decide not to go. It was not worth it, he would complain, he didn't receive enough help from his comrades. He didn't see any progress. I saw that he was filled with bitterness. I understood him well, but I wanted him to go to the meeting where they were waiting for him. So I would sit down next to him and engage him in conversation, caressing him and pleading with him to sweeten his bitterness with work on behalf of his ideal. Sometimes I would bring one of the children to him and with the baby's little hands stroke his face, his hair, and his neck.

"For him, for your son, you must continue your work! Set a good example for him so that he will adopt your ideas." And thus slowly I brought his courage back to him. He would sit himself down, take the child on his lap and play with him. I would go into the kitchen and make supper and he would go out to the meeting.

Once, during this kind of scene, Anna arrived with a good friend. They had come from a meeting where Most had been expected to speak. They found him lying on the sofa, bitter and dejected. He didn't want to go to the meeting in such a bad mood. I was sitting next to him begging him to go. Our guests remained standing and observed us. Later, they looked at each other and began to smile.

"Do you know why we are smiling?" my sister asked me. "There, at the meeting, the comrades said that Most will not come. 'He no longer has any time for us, why should he hurry over when he can spend time at home with his young wife? We will not have him in the movement for long. He has no time for us now.'" Yes, how bitter we were hearing this talk! I was the one who always sent him to his work; I had practically starved while giving him courage and helping him.

Most Refuses to Write For a Capitalist Newspaper and We Suffer Further Need

Freiheit was in a bad state financially. The weekly subscribers paid irregularly. Others had hardships themselves, and some of their other expenses took precedence over paying for *Freiheit*. Naturally, the newspaper suffered greatly because of this. The printer wanted money, paper had to be bought, postage cost money, office rent had to be paid, and there was no money. There was almost nothing left for the family.

When Most had to appear at a meeting he didn't have anything to wear. His black suit was already too old and shiny, so I washed

Johann Most, ca. 1895
(Internationaal Instituut voor Sociale Geschiedenis [Amsterdam])

and ironed it myself using hot water and vinegar, which took out the shine. It was difficult for me to do, but we didn't have any money to pay for this work to be done. When Most would appear in the old, washed suit, I was happy that I was able to help him, even with such a small thing.

The reason why I include these details is to offer an accurate image of Johann Most's life. If he had been someone who could be persuaded, we would not have had to lead such a difficult life. The following instance will confirm this:

One time, shortly after my second son was born, Most came home and showed me a letter that he'd received from the *New York World* (one of the biggest and most popular newspapers in America). The *World* suggested to him that he write a column each week for the Sunday *World*. He could write whatever he wanted and he'd get paid fifty dollars a week. Fifty dollars for one column, that is. He said to me:

"What do you have to say about it, Helene? If I take this on, it would be good for us. You and the children could be somewhat relieved from our ever-present need. You would no longer have to take our old things and remake them into pants and shirts for the children, and I would be able to help the *Freiheit*. Would you want me to take the *World's* offer?"

We both laughed. I knew very well that he would never do it, and he knew that I would never want him to.

"Bravo, my Helene!" he proclaimed. "I knew that you would never ask me to do this." And he good-naturedly added, "Courage, my love! Courage! We will find a way out." We both had tears in our eyes, and laughed off the *World's* offer. It was better this way: our souls remained pure.

A Curious Individual

As I write these lines, I recall something that happened several years ago, not long after Most's death.[89] I had a little candy store in which I slaved to make an extremely poor living for me and my two children. For years, a wholesale stationary salesman would come into the store, and I'd place a small order. He would say that it didn't matter that the orders were so small, that he liked talking with me; it was a change for him from what he dealt with in his regular work. He was sorry that I worked so hard, that I looked so terrible, that I was being buried alive in the store. He didn't know who I was because I used my maiden name—Minkin. I didn't want to drag Most's name into this sort of life.

This man was a bit of a radical, a sympathizer with the radical movement, and a free-thinker. Once when we were speaking about various things, I mentioned the name Most.

"He was a remarkable man, that Most, but a great drunkard," he said. "And also a scoundrel."

"In what way was he scoundrel?" I asked.

"Oh!" he said. "What do you know about Most? I knew him very well. I once met him in Chicago and shook hands with him."

"So," I said, "that must have been a great honor for you. *Nu*, what did you find out about him when you shook his hand?"

"I will tell you: he was a big drunk. He enjoyed life. He published a newspaper called the *Freiheit*. Have you ever heard of the *Freiheit*?"

I didn't answer his question. My throat began to tighten. The salesman continued to speak: "He published a newspaper and wasted his money on drink, and lived a gluttonous life."

Here I must note that Most really didn't drink a lot. He would stand by the bar in a saloon owned by a comrade. They often held meetings in the back part of the saloon, so Most would take a glass of schnapps in hand and stand and talk for hours with this same glass. But he would always be seen holding a glass of schnapps. I recount this not to wash Most clean of sin. No, that is absolutely not necessary. If Most had really drank as much as people say, it wouldn't have been such a great crime. A man who possessed such a passionate temperament as Most, a man who had the power to penetrate into the soul of another human being like Most had—this kind of person must also have other passions.

When I heard how my salesman, who had never lifted a finger for the movement, spoke about Most with such disregard, a feeling of disgust overwhelmed me. And not only for this man alone but for the entire world, for everyone. And he was a freethinker, a radical! This is how you speak about a man who spent over ten years in different prisons, who starved, lived in poverty; wore old clothes, *shmattes*,[90] rags; died in [poverty?]; and left his family in direst need?

"And what became of Most's family?" I asked the salesman. "I believe he left a wife and two young children. I don't think that you have the right to say that Most lived in luxury off the movement's money. I once knew Mrs. Most and was in their house. I saw great poverty. What became of Most's family?"

The man smiled slyly and answered, "You don't have to worry. That Mrs. Most lives much better than you. She doesn't need to slave away like you. See how you look! You'll soon fall down from all this work. And you worry about Mrs. Most! She's enjoying life with the comrades. They do not abandon her."

"And the children?" I asked. "Who looks after the orphans of Johann Most?" In the meantime, my eldest son had come home from school. When he was coming up the stairs that led to our two dark rooms, he stopped abruptly. He heard what was being said about his father and mother, and when he heard that "the comrades are taking good care of her," he made a fist and went back into the store to fight with the man. I, however, wanted to hear more about what these fine "people" had to say about Most and his family; I winked at him to be quiet and he obeyed me. Hot tears began to stream down my face and my chin began to quiver. Most once said in his joking way that he would want to be dead and hear what everyone had to say about him. And there I was, standing and listening to what was said about us both. For this I suffered so many years. For this, Most devoted his entire life!

The man looked at me. He began to understand that something he said had deeply affected me. He sat for a while longer and then left. Later at his club, the salesman asked if anyone knew the family Minkin. They told him that the old Minkin would often come to play checkers in the *kibbetzernye*[91] (a famous café on Division Street at that time—Herrick's Café), and someone else told him that he had played a few times with my father. That Minkin was a fiery one and a fine chess player. A real clever and intelligent man. His daughter had married the old Most.

It is not hard to imagine what the man felt hearing these things. He came and begged me to forgive him. He told me how he had found out the truth.

We Settle in Buffalo

Most told me he had received an offer from some comrades in Buffalo. They wanted to publish a daily labor newspaper and wanted him to be the editor. They will publish *Freiheit* and give him enough for his family; they would pay him fifteen dollars a week.[92] Most was very enthusiastic about the offer. The *Freiheit* could be published regularly. He wouldn't have to wrack his brains like he did for so many years! Here was Most's newspaper—that was his main concern.

The offer didn't appeal to me; my heart told me that no good would come of it. I told Most that I didn't like the plan because he didn't bend to the wills or commands of other comrades. He became very angry with me and didn't take my advice. In his heart Most knew I was right, but he was so anxious about the financial difficulties he encountered publishing *Freiheit*, and he wanted to save it. Nothing else mattered to him.

So he went to Buffalo, while I remained with the children in New York.[93] He'd promised to send me a few dollars to live and he would think about what to do. If he was not able to stay there, he would come back to us, and if he was, he would send for us. He soon wrote to me that he thought the newspaper was successful and that the children and I should come to him. He was living with a stranger and didn't feel comfortable. He wanted to have a proper home and children, so he could give himself up entirely to his work. He wrote that he longed for his "threesome" (that's what he called us, me and the children). Being separated from his family had hindered his activities.

So I took the children, the old furniture, and our old *shmattes*, and went in Buffalo. The "furnishings" arrived in Buffalo before we did and when we got there, the place was already set up. The apartment that Most had rented for us was in an old, dilapidated building; underneath was a candy store that at night became a saloon where there were often parties with music and dancing. The carousing went on all night and it was impossible to sleep. Our place had four rooms with two separate entrances from a little hall. On one side was a huge kitchen [that looked?] like a little dance-hall with black, cracked floor-boards. An old stove stood in the middle of the room. Most [lit?] the stove for us. There was also a pair of chairs, the children's furniture (I bought a set for them), a little table, two chairs, and a rocking chair. All of this was in the great room. The sink was in a dark, little hall. Steps led to the street, which was often buried in [snow?] or covered with ice. I put the children's beds in the bedroom and set up a bed for myself too. On the other side was "the nice house," as Most used to call it. There stood the sofa, bureau, bookshelves, some chairs, and another [bed?]. The floors were covered with straw mats. Most slept in this room. It was very cold in there, and Most called it the "icebox." He would say: "I'm going to sleep in the icebox." The rent was eight dollars a month. He had taken the apartment because it was opposite the editorial office where he worked, and the rent was very cheap.

At night it was very lively, not only from the "cat and mouse" of the candy store but also the place itself: the mice and rats would come out of the floor boards and would dance to the music from downstairs. Once, when I was asleep in the little bed with my braids down, I felt as if someone was pulling at my braid. I was very tired, because I had done the laundry, and it was very difficult to do the wash because I didn't have a washtub in the kitchen. I needed to bring in the wooden washtub from the hall and fill it with water, going back and forth schlepping the hot kettle from the stove. This exhausted me. So I lay in bed half asleep, opening my eyes a little and then quickly shutting them again. I felt my braid being pulled apart more strongly. I sat up. I thought that Most had woken me up and I wanted to [scold?] him for such a joke. As I already mentioned, I was very tired and in a bad mood, but when I opened my eyes I saw a huge rat scampering quickly. The rat had been pulling on my braid. I shuddered, quickly got out of bed, and in fear ran to the children. I heard that rats attack children, so my heart trembled in case the same had been done to them. They were in their beds sleeping. From that time on, I was not able to sleep. I had heard that rats were afraid of light so I kept the lamp on the whole night and watched over the children.

In Buffalo, we lived very economically, and I only needed milk for the children. The milkman came to Most's office to collect for the milk since I rarely had anything on me to pay him. Some good it did him! When the milkman came to collect, even Most didn't have any money. He asked his office to pay him, so one of his managers asked, "What does your wife do with so much milk?" Most told me that with [embarrassment?]. This way of life had already begun to dampen Most's spirit. He told me that the comrades in the office [laughed?] often with him: "What does your wife really think? Does she think she's a countess? And why does she clothe the children in white?"

Life was terrible for me. I didn't have anyone to confide in, except a neighbor who had a little hotel in the next house and a little saloon. She was a very pleasant woman. She would observe me when I stood outside with the two children, still babies. Once she said to me, "Mrs.

Most, I see you standing quietly as you stare at the passersby, at everything that happens, and you remain silent, but your eyes are like open books to me. I see that a great drama is taking place inside you." Yes, this good neighbor of mine had no [illusions?].

Most would work very hard and experienced much unpleasantness from his bosses. They protested that what he wrote was too radical for their organ: the *Arbeiter-Zeitung*. He explained to them that he couldn't write other than what was in his heart and understanding dictated; he must write according to his own convictions. Similarly, with *Freiheit* they didn't want him to write whatever he wanted; the owners had already begun to consider the *Freiheit* their newspaper and were really telling him what to write. Most always took his bitter heart out on the house. Where else could he let out all the anger he had accumulated if not at home?

Most would have a little pleasure when he would go for a walk with his children in the afternoon. He would speak with them on the way. "I feel so good with my sons," he would say. "This is a change from my daily life. The first time in my tumultuous life that I can stroll with my children and live like a normal man." But he wasn't able to enjoy this pleasure every day, for many times he would be so busy that he couldn't come home for lunch. I'd bring hot containers right from the stove so he wouldn't have to go hungry at work.

When Most had to travel for a few days to give lectures, he wouldn't be able to crawl out from under the work that accumulated while he was away. During this time, I stayed alone with the children until late at night. Oh, what bitter thoughts and feelings tormented me in my loneliness! The children would sleep and a terrible silence and loneliness dominated the house, as in a grave. From time to time, the silence was broken by a mouse running by and immediately disappearing under the boards.

This is how we would take baths (Most called it a washpot): I would put big pots of water on the stove. From the hall sink I would drag in the wooden washtub and pour in hot and cold water. Most would get into it on his knees and wash himself. But he was happy; he would say that when a man is clean on the outside he feels clean on the inside.

After bathing, I had to scoop up the water with pots, carry it out into the hall, and pour it out.

I Leave Most and Go Back to New York

I saw that the *Arbeiter-Zeitung* would not exist for long, given all the squabbling, and I was annoyed with this whole way of life, so I decided to go back to New York with my children and work and earn a living for me and my two babies. I could no longer sustain myself on the *Arbeiter-Zeitung*.

However, I didn't have any travel money and I knew that Most wouldn't let me go, so I told him that I wanted to visit my family and asked him whether he could get a ticket for me through the *Arbeiter-Zeitung*. Since the *Arbeiter-Zeitung* had an advertisement and timetable for the railroad, it received a certain number of tickets, which Most would use for his protest trips. He was able to get one for me.

In my heart I knew well that I would never return to Buffalo. Quietly I packed all of his things into a satchel, his underwear and other things. I patched up all of his clothes. "You should have enough until I get back and you shouldn't have to search for it," I told him. I left Buffalo, where I had spent a miserable ten months. I didn't know what I would do or where I would go with the children. My whole family, my father and sister, were poor and didn't have enough to support themselves.

I decided to go to my father and from there determine what to do next. I stayed a little while with my father and my sisters Anna and Rochel. I wrote to Most that I was not going to come back to Buffalo. If he wanted to return to New York, I would help with all my might to get him back on his feet, but if he wanted to stay in Buffalo, he would have to do it alone, without me and the children.

I went to see the comrades and spoke with them. They promised to help publish *Freiheit* again in New York. Most told the comrades in Buffalo that he no longer wanted to work for them; he couldn't sell his soul to them for a bowl of lentils. They told him that if he wanted to leave them, he could not take *Freiheit* with him because it belonged to them now. So he told them that he would go to New York to talk it over with his wife. He left his satchel with the patched-up underclothes with them and came to New York.

Helene Minkin in later life.
(*Jewish Daily Forward* [*Forverts*], December 18, 1932)

Most talked it over with a few committed comrades, and they promised to help so that *Freiheit* would once again be published in New York. They found a young typesetter who was ready to set *Freiheit* at night for free. The printer promised to wait for the money until *Freiheit* was standing securely on its feet. We also received paper on credit. We found a cheap place to live, somewhere deep in Brooklyn. Most set off on a trip.[94] He traveled from city to city, and received a little money at the meetings. Slowly, it can be said, they crawled on all fours until *Freiheit* was once again published in New York. Of course under these conditions we could only lead the poorest of lives.

From all of this misery, I became very ill. I didn't have anyone to help me. Most led me away, with the help of a cane, to Dr. Solotaroff, who gave me electrical treatments.[95]

Most Gets Very Jealous

Most was once again busy entire days and nights with *Freiheit* and this continued for several years until the paper had worked its way up a little.

Once in a while I would think, and even now I still do, about my life with Johann Most, and I ask myself, what kind of "living together" was it, really? Was this the usual, ordinary cohabitation of a man and wife or was it exceptional due to our personalities, the difference in our ages and characters, and also the fact that I was a Jewish girl and he a Christian? And that I didn't know much about the world and Most already knew so much about life and relationships between men and women? Yes, Most had already experienced so much in his life. He observed how the people around him lived, and much of what he saw and observed had taken away his respect and faith in family life and women. I didn't know all of this before; I first found out when we were living together.

And just as the whole world, both near and far, was wondering about us—how I, a young girl, had devoted myself with body and soul to an old man, Most himself wondered about it. Yes, a doubt would sneak its way into Most's heart as to whether I was really faithful and devoted to him. And that was not all. His comrades had spread the poison of doubt through his veins and as a result, scenes of jealousy would take place between us. When Most went away on a long protest trip, or when he was in prison, he would come home and look me in the eyes for a long time. Deep, so deep, he looked inside as if to see my soul—well, I don't know what he really wanted to find there, but it annoyed me, it annoyed me a lot. For I didn't search into his soul as he did in mine. I knew that in every city where he gave lectures at large assemblies there were single and married women who admired his enthusiastic speeches and his deep and fiery blue eyes with which he was able to look into a person's soul. The single and married women stood around him to catch one of his warm smiles. It is obvious that a man with his fiery temperament—he was like a fire-spitting mountain—the temperament with which he had spoken and awakened sleeping souls, would reflect this in his entire being. Naturally, he was passionate in every way. Most would say: "What do you and all the others want? That I should hang on a string from the sky and when I am needed to give a speech or write an article, the string will descend and place me on the platform or put a pen in my hand, and after I've completed my work, the string will pull me up and fine—I am no longer of this earth?"

I was not much bothered by Most's behavior when he was in a strange place. As the saying goes: to understand is to forgive. But I knew and felt that he belonged to us, to me and the children, and that when he was on the road, he thought of us, his "dear three," as he called us. No one could ever take our Johann Most away from us, just as I could never take him away from the masses, from all the suffering, oppressed people, even if I wanted to, though I never wanted to. Only death could do this.

No, I never permitted myself to think that Most belonged only to us, and life was so full of hard work and bitter worries that I didn't have the time or strength to occupy myself with all these questions. Even when Most would tell me about his "conquests," as he would call them, it didn't interest me much.

At a more festive meeting, for example, after he'd returned from a long, cross-country protest trip or when he was released from prison, he would be the big hero. The comrades (male and female) would surround him and I would stay seated alone. (Naturally, I could have also hung around him, but I didn't like to do so because I didn't want to show off that he was my husband, that I had a right to him, that he belonged to me.) When I sat by myself, one of the comrades would sit down and talk to me. Possibly they did this out of a feeling of "comradely" duty, which I neither expected nor desired; possibly out of politeness. Perhaps they thought it made me sad to sit alone and wait until "my man" would be free to come to me. And when a German comrade sits next to a young lady, the wife of the old *rebbe* in fact, he feels a duty to compliment her. From a distance, Most would observe who sat next to me and study the character of our conversations. He considered the expression that the comrade had on his face and my expression, whether I appeared happy, content.

Later, at home, he would let loose his jealousy and resentment. I never wanted to respond to him, and when he would ask whether a comrade had declared his love, I would answer, "of course he did, why not? Don't you think it's possible that someone would be interested in me?"[96] He wouldn't know what to do—whether to believe me or not, whether I was serious or joking.

I Leave Most Because of His Jealousy

At one point he and his jealousy caused me to take the children and leave. What brought me to this step was this: It was a Sunday. Most had a lot of work to do that day in his room and I decided to visit my father, who lived on Grand Street. I dressed both boys in white suits and I myself put on a white dress. It was a lovely summer day. I especially liked to wear white dresses; it looked so fresh and one didn't have to be decked out in expensive things. The whiteness itself adds what poverty has taken away. Most stood in the door of his room closely observing how I was getting ready to go. That same evening, there was a meeting scheduled downtown—the well-known anarchist Isaacs, with whom I was close friends, was speaking.[97]

"A Hebrew anarchist meeting at Military Hall on the Bowery," from *Harper's Weekly*, August 20, 1892. This meeting took place on August 1, 1892 at 193 Bowery. Emma Goldman spoke in defense of Berkman's assassination attempt. Other speakers included Dyer Lum, Francesco Saverio Merlino, and Josef Peukert. Johann Most had denounced Berkman's act a few days earlier.

"Why are you so dressed up just to go to your father?" he asked with irritation. "I know that you are going to the Isaacs-meeting and not to your father, and that's why you are dressing as you do."

This upset me quite a bit. I told him that I had not even thought about going to the meeting, but now I would definitely go, after I saw my father.

"Leave the children if you are going to the meeting," he said angrily. "I'll put them to bed and will spend a little time with them after I've finished my work." So I left the children, telling them that I was going out and they should play outside for a little while and then come up to "papa."

After I had spent a little time with my father I went to the meeting. I met many of my friends and acquaintances there, and after the meeting, we all went to a café for a little while. It was then that I realized how necessary it was for me to stray a little from my lonely path, to change my atmosphere for a while. And although I was uneasy, I lingered and came home quite late.

I found Most circling the room angrily, and we fought. He said things to me that stabbed me right in the heart. I went over to the children, kissed them, and covered them well. Then I said to Most that I would come for the children in the morning, and I left the house. That night I went back and forth on the El, and in the morning I went to my sister's where I slept a little. Then I went home and took the children. I split the furniture with him and rented a couple of little rooms.

Peace Again

Later, when the first flames had died down, we met. He looked terrible.

It was hard for me to see how shabbily he was going around; his suit was dirty and wrinkled and I felt as if I were somehow guilty. "Who will get his suit ready when he has to speak at a meeting?" I asked myself. And we reconciled so that I could once again press and wash his suit and attend to him, and so the children would have him again and he could have the children with him. I knew how much he loved them.

However, the resentment stayed in my heart a long time, and only our new, bitter suffering and hard times made me forget it. I eventually realized that I would not be able to change Most or cure him of his jealousy, so I let it go. Sometimes his jealousy prompted me to tease him a little. For example, when I would get a letter from my sister, who was living in Boston at that time (we would write each other in Russian), I would pretend to quickly hide the letter so he wouldn't see it.

"What kind of letter are you hiding from me?" he asked.

"Nothing, nothing," I answered, pretending to be scared. Then I would take the letter and give it to him. Of course, he couldn't read it, but he would already see that it was from my sister. He would laugh in embarrassment and say, "Oh, you cursed one, you little devil! You Russian czar, you want to tease me? Just wait and I will one day settle the score."

Another time I took Most's old hat, a cane, and one of his cigars, which I lit and let burn a little, then put in an ashtray and went to bed. When Most came home, he stood uneasily and looked around. From the dark room where I was lying, I observed the scene and it took all of my effort to hold it in and not break out into laughter.

"What the hell? Dammit! What is this?" he shouted. "Who is this here? Ach, what the hell?"

He ran quickly over to my bed. I was lying in my clothes. When he came up to me, I burst out laughing. He considered the hat, the cane, and realized that they were all his, so he also laughed heartily, but also became very red. He said, "Wait, wait! I'll get you!" And then he said good-naturedly, "I brought some good cake. Please make some coffee so we can eat and drink."

Once, Most brought me two tickets to a Russian performance of Chirikov's *Yevrei*, which was playing at the Yiddish theater, and put on by the well-known actor Orlianoff and his troupe. It was right after the Kishinev pogrom.[98] Most suggested that I go with my sister, and he would stay at home and look after the children. I was very excited and went to the theater with my sister. When I came home in tears (who didn't cry?), I stood standing in the door completely shocked. I found the house completely turned upside down. The furniture was thrown around, the table, chairs, and sofa stood on end, the dishes were lying on the floor and a few of them were broken. The pictures on the walls and the mirror were turned around. The books from the bookcase were spread all over the ground and the bookcase itself was turned over. The clothes from the dresser were lying on the ground. I didn't have any gas so I looked for a lamp and a match but couldn't find them. I became almost wild. I ran into my room where the children were sleeping, and found them lying quietly and well-covered. I caressed their warm cheeks. Then I went to Most's room and I saw him lying stretched out on his couch, with his head covered up. I threw myself at him in terror and tore off the blanket. I saw a red, laughing face. He was shaking from laughter and grabbed me.

"I once told you that I would play a trick on you! So I made a 'pogrom.'"

Nu, could I be angry at him? This time I had brought the cake, and I told him that today he had to make the coffee. He got up and made coffee, and afterwards helped me put the house back in order. In the morning, the children had no idea what had happened.

"If you are going to fool me again, I will play even worse tricks on you," he said mischievously.

Most, the Man and the Father

When Most and I were in public, I would call him "comrade" (of course I would call him by his first name at home). One time when I was with him I went with my sister who was living with us at the time, to a meeting where Most was the speaker. As always, he spoke very well. The theme was "The Paris Commune," and I was aflame with excitement. Every time he spoke on these themes, he would speak with fire and flames. His fiery eyes looked and set the whole [crowd?] aflame. He sent sparks from his heart into everyone else's. He [looked over?] to me and smiled. I answered him with a smile, and afterwards, on the way home, he began to speak with me. I remembered that I was angry at him so I didn't answer.

He asked, "Why aren't you answering me? Didn't you just smile at me?"

"I smiled at Comrade Most because he is such a good speaker, but I'm still angry at my husband," I answered.

"Would that I was your sister," he said. The three of us laughed and we made up.

I cannot say that life at home for us was like other people's, because circumstances didn't allow it. Mostly I was alone at home with the children. Sundays, when I would sometimes sit in the park with the children, and Most had some work to do or was traveling (he would spend three months a year on his protest tours), I would get very lonely. I felt as if my house was a cemetery and one could bury the dead there. Outside it was beautiful; the sun was warm, the park full of people. Couples, dressed in their Sunday finest, passed by. They gazed in each other's eyes. They murmured sweet, loving things to each other. Families would go by: a father, mother, and children. The father helped the mother take care of the children. I felt one hot tear after another roll down my face. Sometimes I would be standing outside in the dark, and I would look into a lighted room where there would be people living, laughing, dancing, and drinking the elixir of life; I would be standing outside on the threshold.

It would immediately come back to me that I had two dear, fine children whom I was raising so they would become great men. They would be useful for society, understand the world, and help us and our work—is this not great wealth? Is this not enough happiness for me?

Most would come home late, about one o'clock or later. He really wanted me to stay up until he arrived because he always wanted to tell me everything about what he'd done that day or that evening. He would bring me cake and I would make coffee. We would sit up for a few hours.[...] First he would go see the children, put his hand on their cheeks and kiss them, and then he would come see me in the kitchen. The kitchen was our parlor. There he would tell me about his life, his years of wandering, and his experiences in prison. He would often help me patch up his underwear. He told me that sewing patches was his occupation when he was in prison in London. He would also joke and tell funny stories, and we would both roll over in laughter.

One time, Most came home and gave me a huge, heavy ring—a wedding ring. I looked at the present and asked: "What do I need a wedding ring for?"

He told me a whole story. A comrade, someone whom he had never seen before but who said he was a comrade, came to him after the meeting and told him that he was in trouble, his wife was pregnant and there was no money in the house. So he wanted to pawn his wife's wedding ring, which had cost him ten dollars. He wanted only five dollars for it, because he wanted to get it back quickly.

"So I gave him the five dollars," he said. "Wear it in the meantime until the comrade comes to get it."

I put on the ring and knocked on the table with it, "Now I am really married," I said to Most. "But you don't need to be afraid that the comrade will come back to get the ring back. It's copper and worth five cents."

"Ach!" he said. "You think you are so smart with your *yiddishe kop*."[99]

Five dollars! For me, this was like five thousand dollars is to others. I would have been able to buy two pairs of shoes for my boys, I thought to myself. I was certain that he had been tricked, as often happened. Most was as naïve as a child and not schooled in everyday life. The next day I went to a pawnshop and asked how much he would give me for the ring. The man took the ring in his hand, looked it over, and then looked at me. Eventually he said, "This ring is not worth more than ten cents."

When Most got home, I told him what the man in the pawnshop had said. He knocked himself on the head and said, "Oh, how stupid I am. I am truly a *goyisher kop*."[100] I used to say to him that when it came to normal, practical life, he had a *goyishen kop*. Anyone who wanted to fool him could.

Most loved his children very much and when they were still babies, he would ask me to put them in bed with him. "I want to have 'office hours' with my boys," he'd say. He would usually come home around lunchtime, and he'd sit in his room and write while I prepared the meal. When the children were home and began to get rambunctious, I'd ask him to help me keep them quiet. He would quickly get himself to work, grabbing a brush and a hand towel, and chasing after the children, beating them with both. They would take all the pillows off the beds and throw them at him. Soon they would be rolling around on the floor making so much noise that I would have to shout at them to stop. Because of that they called me "the cop." "Be quiet, children, the cop is here!" he would say. He would laugh until tears ran down his face. Poor Most had only now, at an advanced age, enjoyed that which he was unable to in his younger years.

If Most came home early in the evening, when the children were still awake, he would spend time with us. He was like a guest for the children, who were usually asleep when he came home. They'd beg me to let them stay in the kitchen a bit longer than usual. Then Most would sing and recite. This gave me intense joy. Even today, when I think about those moments, I can hear his recitations in my ears. I also loved when he would tell stories, as he always told them so well.

Otherwise life for us was the same as for many other impoverished laborers, often bitter and disappointing. To me, it seems that, in general, life was a means to an end. That is, one ate—if there was anything to eat—and slept, so that one could live; and lived, so that one could work and struggle and raise two sons, imbue them with our spirit, and prepare them as our inheritors who would continue our struggle to liberate the suffering.[101]

The Assassination of President McKinley

Later (in 1901) Leon Czolgosz, a Pole, assassinated McKinley, the president of the United States at the time. At first, no one knew who Czolgosz was and what had driven him to this deed. As was to be expected, people immediately began to persecute the leaders of the

John Jr. and Lucifer Most, sons of Helene Minkin and Johann Most.
(*Jewish Daily Forward* [*Forverts*], December 11, 1932)

anarchists, Most and Emma Goldman. It just so happened that a week before the assassination, Most had been very busy and didn't have time to write an editorial for *Freiheit*, so he printed an article from a certain anarchist named Heinz [sic]. In the article, written fifty years earlier, the writer expressed his opinion that there would come a time when people had to free the world of tyrants.[102]

So because he reprinted the article, people considered Most responsible for the assassination. He was arrested at a picnic on Long Island, while he and other comrades were singing revolutionary songs.[103] The picnic was scattered. He sat in prison several weeks, but at the examination in court, the judge had to release him because they couldn't come up with a charge against him. He was immediately arrested again at a meeting in New York, along with McGuinn, a young English anarchist, and he sat in prison for a couple of weeks. They wanted to hold him while they figured out what to do with him in regards to Czolgosz's assassination of McKinley. Eventually Most was arrested for the Heinz [sic] article, which he had published in *Freiheit*, and he was sentenced to a year in prison.[104] They immediately shaved his beard, as they always did when he was put in prison. Three months before his release they would let him grow it back.

However, this time, Most's lawyer appealed the case to the higher courts.[105] He was granted what is called a "stay of proceedings," that is, he was released on bail until the higher court made a decision. Most had to come out of prison without his beard and with his misshapen face, so it was scary to look at him. It especially pained us (him and me) that the children had to see him this way. The children were afraid when they saw him for the first time without a beard. I told them the whole story of their father's childhood and his illness.

It became impossible for us to remain in Brooklyn, where we were living at the time, because people hounded us as soon as we showed ourselves on the street.[106] They threw stones at us and called us horrible names. They would shout after us: "There goes the family of the leader of the gang that killed President McKinley!" Stones flew from all directions. No one stopped this. In school, the bigger kids beat our children and called them all kinds of names. Once my youngest son came home with a swollen face from the smacks he had gotten from the other kids.[107] I fled to the Bronx and took a place under the name of Miller. We had often used that name to protect the children, and under that name I enrolled them in school. Of course I didn't bring the transfer documents from the Brooklyn school to the new school, so I said that I had lost the transfer. In the meantime, they enrolled the children and I promised to get another transfer for them, which naturally, I didn't get.

After Most's beard had grown back, and the bare ugliness was once again hidden, he was taken to prison. The appeal wasn't accepted and the higher court found him guilty of inciting murder, based on that article. His beard was once again shorn.[108] The bondsman, a German comrade named Albinger, a few of the comrades, and I went with Most to court in the morning to deliver him to the wolves.[109] My heart bled for him, but of course I couldn't show it. Most pretended to be happy and told jokes. He gave the *Freiheit* (the business end) over to me entirely.

"Be strong," he said to me. "It won't be so easy for you to lead the struggle alone, but hold *Freiheit* tight in your hand, and under no circumstances hand my 'beloved daughter' (this is what he always called the *Freiheit*) over to anyone." As an answer, I silently pressed his hand and in my heart I resolved that no such thing would ever happen to the *Freiheit*.

In court, I held myself back and didn't display any distress. When we went up the courthouse's high stairs, we saw a large gang, who began shouting: "There he is, the murderer, the bomber! Hang him! Hang him!" And they made a drawing of a noose.

"Blind sheep!" Most said, with a bitter smile, and we took him quickly into court. When he was taken away, he passed the bench where I was sitting. I went up to him, pressed his hand and said quietly, "Goodbye, Johann."

After that I went quickly to my dear friend with whom I had left the children. My head ached terribly and I wanted to lie down as soon as possible. I met up with my sister Anna there. The evening papers had already been delivered, and they described the terrible scene that played out in court, when Most was led away to prison. I fell on my knees, according to the English newspapers, my hair fell loose, and I kissed Most's hand and screamed "Goodbye!"[110]

My sister and friend looked at me with questioning glances. "Is this true?" my sister asked.

"What do you think? Is it true?" I responded. I told them what really happened as we parted in court.

New Troubles, New Suffering

Most was back in prison and I stayed with the children and *Freiheit*. Once again we struggled to get by—not only for us, but also for *Freiheit*. The comrades established a committee, which decided to give me ten dollars a week for the children and me to live on, to provide Most with food in prison, and also to pay "Uncle" (this is what we called the man who would bring us an article from Most every week). Uncle had easy access to the prison, so we'd give him a few dollars, as well as schnapps and wine from the comrades.

I visited Most every month, bringing with me a large satchel with all kinds of canned goods, fruit, chicken, and sausages. After that, there was six dollars a week left for rent and for me and the children to live on. I took in boarders, and we managed. We were already accustomed to poverty and need.

❧ ❦

I remember a funny incident: My sister Anna was very artistic. She loved everything that was beautiful; she didn't like faded colors or patched up clothing. Even when we were children, when my mother would patch our dresses, Anna wouldn't wear them. It didn't bother me so much; I only wanted my dresses clean and in one piece—patched was fine.

Once Anna came over and saw that my little boy was wearing a pair of patched and faded pants, she said, "Oh, Helene, give those pants away to a poor child already."

"I already gave the pants to a very poor child," I answered. "I cannot find a poorer child than mine." We both laughed bitterly.

❧ ❦

Winter came—a hard winter with new and more challenging troubles. I became seriously ill—with a lung infection—but overcame it.

Most suffered greatly with not being able to see his children, but at the same time he didn't want them to see him at the prison, in convict's clothes and with a shaven face. They were still too young to understand that their father was a martyr for his ideal and not some thug. They would see him as an inmate, humiliated and insulted, with his misshapen face, and it would make a negative impression on them. "If I only had a picture of them I would hang it on the wall and look at them all the time, my dear little boys," he would say to me when I visited. So I brought him a picture of our two sons.

He grabbed the photo from me, and laughing hysterically, he began to kiss it. Tears ran down his cheeks. The prison attendant came over. Taking the photo, he said in a stern tone, "These kinds of things are not allowed in prison."

"What kind of crime is it to have a picture of your own children on the wall?" I asked.

The man became a little agitated and said, "Ask the warden. Maybe he'll make an exception for you; I don't have the power to allow it."

"Fine, I'll go ask him," I said, and I went straight to the warden across the long prison courtyard. The warden was alone. He looked at me in astonishment.

"Do you see this picture?" I asked him, handing him the photo. He looked at it. "Yes, I see two beautiful boys. So, what do you want?"

"These are my two sons," I explained to him, "Johann Most's two sons. They are very dear to him, and he'd like very much to have this picture on the wall of his cell so he can look at them. I came to ask for your permission. You know that he is not a thug. Do this for him!"

He looked at me and smiled. "Fine, you can give it to him. But how does it happen that you, such a young woman, could be so devoted to such an old man?"

"He is my comrade. You can't understand that right now," I answered him and ran quickly to give Most the photograph. He looked very happy, so I came away from that visit with a good feeling.

❧ ☙

The *Freiheit* was in a good financial situation. I vigorously demanded repayment of obligations through letters and notices published in *Freiheit*, and money came in. In terms of content, *Freiheit* was also in good order; we found a comrade to help with the issues and many others made literary contributions. The lead articles we received

John Jr. and Lucifer Most, two sons of Helene Minkin and Johann Most, 1907.
(Internationaal Instithuut voor Sociale Geschiedenis [Amsterdam])

every week from Most, written in prison and signed "Ahasuerus,"[111]
were interesting and full of fire.

One time, a young man at a meeting asked me, "Who is this
Ahasuerus who writes in the *Freiheit*? You know, Mrs. Most, I always thought that only Most could write with such fire and flames.

Whoever is writing the lead articles in the *Freiheit* now writes as well as Most; many times he writes even better with more sharpness and intensity. Who is it?"

I smiled in my heart and answered, "He doesn't want to be known just yet. He wants to wait until Most is released from prison. Wait, and when he is released, and there's a welcome reception for him, the author will definitely be there. At that point I'll introduce you to him."

"He must be a lot younger than Most, eh?" he asked further. "His writing sounds so fresh."

"Wait," I said. "You'll soon see."

Most was released, and we had a welcome gathering for him.[112] After Most gave a passionate speech, the same young man came to me: "*Nu*, is Mr. Ahasuerus here? Will you introduce me to him?"

"Definitely!" I said. I led him over to Most. "Johann, this young man wants to become acquainted with Mr. Ahasuerus, who wrote the lead articles in *Freiheit* while you were in prison. Most laughed.

"Oh, you scoundrel!" he said to me, and shook the man's hand. The man now understood who Ahasuerus was.

Most is Released From Prison

When Most was released from prison, I gave him back the *Freiheit* along with its money. He was thrilled with my management of the newspaper and said that it had been ages since it was in such a good financial position. Previously, when he went to prison and left *Freiheit* in strange hands, he would return to find the whole thing overturned.

He gave me twenty-five dollars. "Go and buy something with it: a nice dress or whatever you want for yourself." So I went to a store and bought two good wool blankets and a lovely couch-cover. I'd wanted wool blankets for a while; Most really needed them for his rheumatism, and the children needed them too.

❧ ❦

The children had no idea what was happening as we stood at the 29th Street pier waiting for Most to be released from prison.[113] I had told them that he was in Chicago, and that I was sending him all kinds of canned goods that he liked and couldn't get there.

It was a fine, mild early-April morning. We stood by the water and I looked across to the other shore. From a distance I could see the prison buildings, the big courtyard, and the warden's office. I saw two figures coming out of the office, setting off toward the river, where a little boat was standing. They sat down in the boat, and it began to float closer and closer to us. I pointed the boat out to the children and shared the news that it was their father coming from Chicago—really, it was Johann in the company of a prison guard. And thus Most was back by our side!

Most hadn't seen the children for the whole ten months that he was behind bars, and he was very anxious to see them. At the same time though, he didn't want me to see his weakness and his tears. It's a strange character trait that men have; they are ashamed of their human feelings. I turned around to give him an opportunity to rejoice with the children undisturbed. Tears ran down his cheeks as he picked them up one after the other and kissed them and pressed them to his heart. Most didn't want to go home right away. He wanted to celebrate his freedom alone with his family, so I gave him money and we went to the hippodrome.[114] The children had never been there before. From there, we went to a restaurant and then home. We immediately went out again; he didn't want to stay between doors and walls. We went to the saloon where the comrades were waiting for us.

A few days later, after Most's welcome-home party, where he gave a magnificent speech, we were conversing at home and I suggested that he write his memoirs.[115] He had always wanted to, and I thought now was the best time to do it because everything was well-arranged: I could run the *Freiheit* with the help of a few comrades, like I had been doing, and Most would only have to write his feature-articles. He could sit at home and write his book, I suggested. I'd go into the office every day for him and look after everything until he finished his book. Of course, he would continue to give talks and meet with his comrades, but he wouldn't spend time on other things. During the day he could sit and write. Most was very enthusiastic about this idea and that same day I prepared the front room where it was light and airy and he could work comfortably.

Most thought it would be better if he published his work in pamphlet-form, calculating that he could publish twelve leaflets, eighty sides each. He'd publish them one after the other, with the money he received from selling one pamphlet going to the cost of printing the second, and so on. I was very much against this; my heart told me that this wouldn't work. If the first pamphlets didn't sell, it would hurt him and take away his motivation to continue writing. And even if it worked, the preparation each time would take so much energy that he wouldn't be able to work calmly. But he didn't listen to me and did what he thought. I was very busy taking care of the house, keeping him comfortable, and running back and forth to the printer, here with an article, there with something else. [If only?] he had executed it with more certainty, if he'd done what I suggested, and written and published the whole book at once.

He finished the first booklet, printed it, and sent it out to be sold. The comrades bought it, but it didn't go so well and, as I had predicted, it took away some of his courage. He sat himself down again to write. He published the second pamphlet and it also sold slowly. It's possible that it was because of timing: it was still soon after the Czolgosz assassination, and the movement hadn't yet completely freed itself from the consequences of anarchist persecution. The reaction still raged. It's possible that if he had written it in English instead of German, it would have done better. The blood poured out of my heart because I saw how they stabbed Most's heart with knives: I saw how pained his soul was that people showed very little interest. His writing soon began to go slowly. He wrote five booklets, but only four were published—the fifth one wasn't because he died soon after.

Most's last few years after getting out of prison were extremely difficult for him in every way. He fought bitterly with the circumstances. His comrades watched from a distance, not wanting to offer to help him because he didn't let them intervene too much in his work. He didn't let them determine how *Freiheit* was run. Most became very weak physically, but he worked all the more diligently. All of a sudden, he was old before his time. Whenever he was supposed to go to a protest meeting, he wouldn't want to leave the house.

I took a course in obstetrical nursing and massage and began to help raise our material situation. When I finished the course, I made a sign and hung it outside and started to get the house ready so I could practice. Most had to travel on a protest tour, so I wanted [to wait to begin my practice?] until he came back from his trip. I had to help in the *Freiheit* office when Most was not at home.

Most Forbids a Banquet in His Honor

Most was then X [*sic*] years old.[116] The comrades wanted to plan a banquet for his birthday, but he didn't want it and so nothing came of it. Instead, they arranged a big meeting. I didn't feel very well and didn't want to go; I was in a bad mood, because they had let Most suffer so much. He looked so old and so white, and the future was so hopeless. I thought about the old veteran, about the children. What would become of them? How would I be able to give them a proper education? I went downtown with Most, but I went to visit my sister, not to the meeting. I told Most that I'd come later to say goodbye, because he was going straight from the meeting to Philadelphia and from there to places further across the country.

I hadn't been at my sister's long when two comrades arrived, relating what had happened: right before Most finished his speech, he was dragged from the platform and arrested. I went to him at once, and found him sweating and very agitated. Hot sweat was pouring from him. He was put in a cell and released in the morning. When I came back in the morning, he was feeling terrible. He had perspired the entire night in his wet clothes. I begged him to come home with me so he could take off his damp clothes and warm up and dry off his body. I knew that if he followed me, he'd get better and we'd have him with us for a long time. But he didn't take me up on my suggestion.

"How could I do that?" he asked. "You know that the meetings are already arranged in each city and I have to be there at a certain time. I don't want to disappoint them. No, it cannot be put off."

Most's Last "Goodbye"

I went with him to the train.

"Goodbye, Helenche! Be brave and kiss my dear boys for me." And he went. My heart told me that something was going to happen. I went home to the children. I continued to be very busy with the *Freiheit*, and with the house and the children.

Most wrote to me from the road, saying that he didn't feel well, and that he considered cutting short his trip and coming home. When he felt better, he would resume it. He wrote that it was raining when he arrived in Philadelphia and he got soaked again. And at the meeting, he was again dragged from the platform and arrested, and again had to spend the whole night wearing his wet and heavy clothes, and he perspired profusely.[117] In other cities, the same thing happened: he felt terrible and thought about coming home right after he spoke in Cincinnati and Chicago.

I quickly began to clean the house and put everything in order for his return. It was a Saturday. On Fridays I would get the *Freiheit* work ready for the week, and Saturday I'd stay at home. I was almost done with the housework; I had sent the children out to the park and I began to paint the floor in the front room—a job I would often do by myself. I was lying on the floor slowly guiding the brush over the boards and I couldn't stop thinking about Most. He was sick, alas, and what would happen now? And who knew how he was doing out there, away from home. Perhaps he was feeling terrible and here I was painting the floor. It broke my heart. Somewhere a clock struck twelve. I got up quickly from the floor and began to run around the house like a crazy person. I got dizzy. I stopped and began to listen. It seemed to me that someone was calling me, someone was crying. I went around restlessly until the children returned from the park to eat lunch. Mechanically, I made something to eat and sent them back to the park. Mechanically, I washed the dishes and sat myself down, and right after that I became absorbed in a dream.

The Heart-Breaking Telegram About Most's Death

Someone knocked on the door.

"Come in!"

Hayes, the printer, a very good friend of Most's and mine, came in.[118] He had never been to our house before; we would meet at the print shop. Usually, he was a tall, pale man. Now he was even paler, and his eyes were full of tears. He stayed standing by the door, staring at me silently. I was afraid to ask him why he had come. He raised his hand toward the ceiling and his teary eyes also gazed upward, toward the sky (he was religious). I understood immediately. He then handed me a telegram from Cincinnati. I read over the few words:

Johann passed away 12:00 at noon. Inform Helene.

At first glance I didn't understand what that meant. My ears rang with the words: "Johann passed away 12:00 at noon."

"'Passed away,' 'passed away,' what does that mean?" Hayes looked at me with his teary eyes. I saw fear in his expression, and I got the idea. "Oh! I understand now, I understand now!" I said. "'Passed away'! Johann has died! He is no longer here."[119]

The children came in and I told them that they no longer had a father. They didn't understand what was happening. Hayes was still there, and soon my sister came. Hayes waited until I was ready to go to Cincinnati. We decided to bring Most back to New York, which is why I didn't bring the children with me. The journey to Cincinnati cost a lot of money, but Hayes had brought some with him and took me to the station.[120] My brother-in-law took the children to my sister Rochel's until I came back.

I traveled that entire Sunday. Many passengers traveling in my car were dressed in their Sunday best. They talked and laughed and read newspapers. I also bought a newspaper, and found the news about the death of the great Johann Most. I read the account in the paper and it occurred to me that a great man had died, a certain Johann Most. I couldn't get used to the idea that *my* Johann Most, the father of my sons, my friend and teacher had died. My thoughts flew by, faster than the train. The father of the German American anarchist movement was dead. A great martyr had passed. Well, he would not have to suffer and worry and struggle; he would no longer have to wrack his brains about how to get money for *Freiheit*; he would not have to go to prison on Blackwell's Island anymore. His beard would not be shaved off and he would not be displayed like a rare animal for the prison visitors. At that moment I didn't want to give an account of what Most meant to me, what role he played in my life. I wanted to go, to go—to keep on going and never arrive anywhere. And at the same time I was burning to arrive, to see with my own eyes if he was really dead.

I arrived in Cincinnati at night, and the comrades were waiting for me at the station. Most had died at the home of the Krauses, a pair of older men who were very committed comrades, and with whom he would always stay when he came to Cincinnati. When I got to the Krauses' house, they led me to the room where Most's dead body was lying. I went in and looked at him. He looked terribly tired and black.

The Krauses told me what had happened: Most arrived on Monday morning, and after greeting them warmly, he asked if he could

Helene Minkin in later life.
(*Jewish Daily Forward* [*Forverts*], December 18, 1932)

lie down because he didn't feel well. They made up a bed for him. He didn't want anything to eat. He told them that for the whole trip, from New York on, the police had harassed him and disrupted every meeting. Each time, he got very upset and perspired terribly in his clothing, which would then dry on his body and cause him to catch a bad cold. When he was asleep, the brothers noticed that his face was red and his breathing was labored, so they called a doctor immediately. The doctor concluded that Most had a rash on his face, but he was mistaken. Most became very ill. When the doctor came again the next day, he immediately saw that his patient was much worse, and when he heard that Most had gone out into the yard at night (Most was very polite and didn't want to wake his hosts), he whistled and said that Most was dangerously ill and he didn't think that he could be saved.

Most lapsed into a high fever. His entire face swelled up and he couldn't see. He didn't go blind, as was mistakenly reported. The swelling had closed his eyes.

"Go and get my Helenche!" he begged his comrades in his feverish state. He gave them our address and told them that it was above a butcher shop. He really thought he was in New York.

"Bring my Helene, she will make me healthy again." He quickly jumped from one thought to the next. He thought that his bed was the train and that he was traveling to Chicago. The train went so slowly and he began pushing the train to go faster.

"Oh," he sighed, "how slow this train is going. I will be too late for the meeting!" Eventually he lost his patience and jumped out of bed in order to run to Chicago. He bumped into something and cut his forehead because he couldn't see where he was going. Then he sat down in the Morris chair, sighed heavily, and it was over.

We wanted to bring him back to New York, and I telegraphed my sister to prepare the house. There would be a huge procession. But the police forbade us from sending Most's body to New York, on the grounds that the rash he died from indicated a contagious illness. The negotiations continued for four days to no avail. We couldn't bring him to New York and the children couldn't see him. We were distraught that the children wouldn't be able to say good-bye to their father.

When I saw how Most was lying in the Krauses' kitchen, between the stove, sink, and washtub—it was impossible to bring the coffin into the main room because the doors were too narrow—I thought that everything in Most's life and death was symbolic: born illegitimately due to poverty; raised in poverty; lived all his years in poverty and need; sat in prison for years; lived with his family in poverty; and died in the middle of his struggle for his ideal, far from his home and family. And here he was in the Krauses' kitchen between the sink and the washtub.

He was laid in a coffin, and dressed in the black suit jacket in which he used to give his speeches. His hands were folded and an expression of contentment had hardened on his face. It seemed as if he had heaved a sigh from a hard day of work and laid himself down to rest. It reminded me of when I visited him on Blackwell's Island and brought him the picture of his children. Oh, how happy he was with it! I so much wanted to do something for him—this last time, here, as he lay in his coffin. I carried a broach with a picture of our sons. The picture was done with natural colors and they looked very good, as though in real life. Most loved that picture very much; he would often gaze at it. So I took off the brooch and pinned it to his jacket lapel. I gave him something to take along with him. I myself don't know why I did it. At that moment, I could offer no rationale. I didn't know what was going on around me, but my desire to still do something for him dictated that I do it.

Back in New York With Johann Most's Ashes

When I got back to New York, I brought a huge trunk with flowers from the funeral and a box with Most's ashes.[121] That was all that remained from my whole life and struggle with him, aside from my two dear children who had gone to school. I spent the whole day sitting in the room where Most used to work. Mechanically, I provided food and whatever else the children needed, and then sat like a stone. It was quiet in the house, quiet like a cemetery. No one visited me the entire week. The children played in the park. They came and went. The days passed and nights arrived. It was dark in the house. The shadows encircled me, and I sat all by myself. No one came, not my family, not the comrades.

The comrades did organize a big gathering to mourn Johann Most. I didn't get involved with that, and when Emma Goldman said that "Johann Most's wife was against her speaking at this gathering," it was of course untrue.[122] I had nothing at all to do with the gathering. But she had to recall the incident with her horsewhip.

The question emerged as to what to do with the *Freiheit*. Many comrades thought we should continue to publish, others were against it. I was against it, and stated this explicitly in a letter that I published in the *Freiheit* on April 21, 1906. I will transcribe a large part of the letter here:

Comrades:

From all sides and from around the whole country, I have received letters in which comrades ask me about the continued publication of the *Freiheit*. They ask me if the *Freiheit* will continue to appear or go under. A few comrades express their opinion and wish that the *Freiheit* keep being published; others are against it, feeling that the *Freiheit* should perish along with its founder. Others think that I should continue the *Freiheit* and become its publisher and that would be a means for our livelihood. I know that capable comrades could be found to deliver the literary side of the newspaper. Everyone means well and I want to use this opportunity to thank everyone from the depths of my heart.

Comrades, I have decided to let *Freiheit* die on the following basis: In the entire world, there is no one who knows better or even as well as I do how much pain the *Freiheit* caused Johann Most, what a bitter struggle he led for *Freiheit*'s existence; how much sacrifice, humiliation, disappointment, poverty, need, and hard work he endured so the newspaper could be published. For Most, *Freiheit* was never just a means to live, as many comrades said of him. On the contrary, Most lived so that he could publish *Freiheit*.

How upsetting it was for him when his comrades insinuated that when they paid for their subscriptions, they were supporting him with it. He never knew whether some of the comrades got the *Freiheit* because they were interested in the ideal or because they wanted to help support its publisher. Most worked very hard in his later years; he worked until his bitter end. He never thought about his own health. I helped to get *Freiheit* out; to shrink the editions, we [ran?] the newspaper ourselves. We often had to work until late at night. At work, he would frequently sigh from exhaustion and disappointment. He knew that no one understood him. I stood next to him and did everything with him. I knew well what was in his heart and in his soul. I

John Jr. and Lucifer Most, sons of Helene Minkin and Johann Most.
(*Jewish Daily Forward [Forverts]*, November 20, 1932)

understood him and helped him swallow his disappointment and bitterness; I helped him carry his heavy cross.

There was often a crisis. *Freiheit*'s financial situation was under such strain that it appeared the paper would go under. I saw how his heart broke. His life had grown together with the *Freiheit*. I think it's symbolic that Most died not in his own home in the lap of his family; he died in the middle of working on behalf of his ideal. He died as he lived: a beautiful and noble death in the field of action. He didn't belong to his family, only to the oppressed. And I, who shared in the bitter struggle with him, feel and think the way he felt and thought, and will act the way Most would have wished me to. If I had his pen and could continue his work, I would do so. No one else can do it; therefore the *Freiheit* must cease to exist. Most and I would often talk about it. He was of the opinion that *Freiheit* should not continue without him. He also believed that his comrades would feel it was their duty to help raise his children. I said that I would not want this. The comrades never forgave Most for claiming the right to start a family for himself, for longing for a little personal joy in life.[123]

I again wrote to the comrades through the anarchist *Freiheit*:

Perhaps I was not strong enough when the storm broke out around me; it was often too much, too difficult to bear. I was still so young, and life had brought me nothing but suffering. My young spirit knew it. Now, however, I feel stronger and I want to raise Johann Most's children myself.

On the question of whether to hand the *Freiheit* over to the group, I have the following to say: Most never permitted others to lead; he conducted his struggle alone. It's enough to recall that the comrades often blamed Most for the *Freiheit* losing too much money. They meant to say that Most spent too much. They also complained that he was too despotic; he didn't allow anyone to check the books and other such things. The last time *Freiheit* was financially at risk, the comrades observed Most's desperation from afar but didn't do anything.

He came to me with the books and the mailing list. He threw them on the table, saying in distress, "Tear it up! Burn everything! The *Freiheit* is devouring too much. I'm done! I'm done!" He placed his arms on the table and threw his head in his hands and his whole body trembled from sobbing. I stood next to him, watching, and my heart broke. He became ill. I ran to our good friend, Hayes the printer, and told him everything. We put together a paper from different articles and published it. That surprised Most. I promised him that from then on I would help support his beloved *Freiheit*, and I did this and maintained the *Freiheit* until his last breath. I fulfilled my duties and I can go. I am convinced I am filling Most's wish, when I say that the *Freiheit* should die along with him. If the comrades want to publish another paper in place of it I wish them luck with this undertaking. But the *Freiheit* is done! I have the feeling that I am acting according to Most's wish.

The comrades didn't care and pressured me to give them all the *Freiheit* material: the subscription lists; the books, and also [postage?] for second class mail. I did it because I wanted some rest, so I could live calmly and find a way to make a living for me and my children.[124]

The *Freiheit* didn't last for long. She could not live without her heart, without her soul. It was re-established by a group, and they chose an editor, a bookkeeper, etc. They collected the debts; they went around to various groups and asked for help, collected money. They schlepped the *Freiheit* around until it eventually died.

They didn't worry much about us, aside from collecting a hundred dollars for us. I really didn't want to take it but did so because of the children. In the beginning, the comrades talked about us, saying that they might do something for the children, for their education. There were even comrades who were of the opinion that the children needed to be taken away from me and raised properly, "anarchistically," as it should be. A good friend, an active comrade, came and told me this. She [knew?] because she would often come to our house and knew the most of anyone what was going on with us. I smiled and reassured her. They had entirely lost the power to do anything to me, these comrades. I knew well that they would stew a little and then forget everything. And just as they hadn't worried about our difficult struggles while Johann Most was alive, so they'd now forget that

Most had given up his life for his ideals, which were also theirs. Most didn't have the opportunity to raise his two dear sons; the duty of both father and mother falling on my weak shoulders. I didn't want others to get involved.

I started to think about how to make a living for the children and, since I had studied to be a masseuse, I decided to pursue it professionally. But it turned out differently than I expected. I hung up a sign saying that I gave massages, manicures, and scalp treatments, all at discount prices.[125] I couldn't spend any money to make a fancy parlor.

Men started to come to me. These customers had no idea who I was—they were "half-comrades," somewhat sympathetic with our ideas. As it turned out, they didn't even begin to understand our principles; they had heard something about anarchists practicing free love, so they thought that massage was just the beginning of it. I didn't insult my customers, but rather calmly explained to them that I only gave massages to women, not men, and only on the recommendation of a doctor. I immediately realized my mistake and decided to take up something else. I sold what little I had and moved in with my father; I began working in a (shirt)waist-shop as an operator. From time to time I would give massages.

Once again things didn't go as I expected, so I bought a little candy store. The store's previous owner tricked me, and instead of bringing in eighty dollars a week, as he had assured me it would, the store brought in fifty. When I asked him why he had swindled me—a poor widow—he answered, "You can bear it. The comrades will give you additional money, but I have no one who will give me any."

"Your children still have a father, and mine don't!" I exclaimed. But what good did my words do?

I toiled in the store, from dawn until midnight, seven days a week. I didn't leave the store for three years. It was as if I were in prison; no one ever visited me. The children and I lived apart from everyone. When I was to go to my children's graduation, it was a special occasion for me—as it would be for every mother whose child completes public school or high school.[126] I began to prepare for the event, readying my dress, my hat, my shoes. Only—the shoes were too narrow for my swollen feet; the hat—too old-fashioned. So I stretched the shoes, re-trimmed the hat, and fixed up the dress. When I went out into the street, I had difficulty walking on the sidewalk, since I had grown unaccustomed to walking with all my time spent in the store. My children took me under their arms and walked with me as if with a child who was being taught to take her first steps. The years went by with new stores, new work, new poverty, until the children finished college and became men.

Often, when I come home tired from work and shut myself up in my room, I relive the moments from our joyous years of struggle. When my eyes rest on the box with Johann Most's ashes, I want to speak with him again. I have the feeling that if I were to open the box, I would see him in there—Most and also myself. I look around—my room is dead silent. The walls seem to be closing in, becoming narrower around me. Soon the walls will come together and swallow me up.

Most's Last Letter

I'll close my memoir with Most's last letter to me from Cincinnati:

March 13, 1906.

My dearest Helene!

You cannot imagine how anxious I've been that I haven't been able to send you any money until now.

Everything had gone in such a way that, until now, my trip wasn't a success.

What little money I received was eaten up by the trains and the halls.

Yesterday, my throat and head ached terribly the whole day and night. My throat is all swollen.

I perspired the entire night. Today I did what I could and I think I'm already a little better. Fortunately, the illness is external and I won't become hoarse (he only worried about whether he'd be able to give his speeches). Today I have to appear at a gathering, though I am sick.

Tomorrow I have to go to Chicago, but I'll travel by day because I haven't slept for four nights on the trains, traveling around sweating profusely; this is what brought me to the point of collapse.

Thursday I will speak in Chicago at the great hall and other meetings will be arranged, so I will be able to send you a little money.

I hope that your health is better than mine.

In the next issue of the paper (*Freiheit*), you'll be able to see how my trip went.

Give my best to the dear boys.

Yours,
Hans

ENDNOTES

1   *Jewish Daily Forward.*

2   There is some confusion as to when their common-law marriage occurred. Common-law marriages, legal in the State of New York until 1938, allowed a couple to marry by contractual consent without ceremonials by a church, clergy, judge, or visit to city hall. John Most, Jr., the couple's first child, was clear that "they were never, of course, formally married." On her petition for citizenship in 1934, Minkin stated that she and Most married on July 15, 1893. Indeed, the census taker in 1900 recorded that they had been married for seven years. The confusion begins when, as early as July 1891, references to a "Mrs. Most" (*Frau Most*) appear in *Freiheit*. Readers were asked to contribute to a defense fund for Most who had been sent to prison on Blackwell's Island. A list of donors appeared in the paper. In July 1891, some donations were listed separately for the benefit of "Frau Most." This would imply that Minkin and Most were married two years earlier than stated in Minkin's own petition. Minkin herself does not provide an exact date of marriage in her memoir. In 1934, Minkin was sixty-one and may not have remembered everything clearly; in fact, she incorrectly identified the ship (*Pocketford* instead of *Wieland*) that brought her to America and the day of entry in New York (June 4 instead of May 31). It is also possible that the term "Frau Most" was used loosely and may not have implied marriage. In that sense, the person in question may not have been Minkin, but Lena Fischer, an activist and the sister of Haymarket defendant Adolph Fischer, with whom Most had an unmarried relationship at least since 1886. She is described in the press as Most's "mistress," or "girlfriend." It was in her apartment at 198 Allen Street (not far from Schwab's saloon) that Most went into hiding in May 1886 and was eventually arrested there. One report had the two travel to Chicago just before Haymarket and return to New York on the day before the bombing. See Paul Avrich's interview with John Most, Jr. on October 28, 1979, in Paul Avrich, *Anarchist Voices: An Oral History of Anarchism in America* (Oakland: AK Press, 2005), 18–

19. For Minkin's Petition of Citizenship, see Ancestry.com. *U.S., Naturalization Records—Original Documents, 1795–1972 (World Archives Project)*, http://www.ancestry.com/. Original records are at *Naturalization Records for the U.S. District Court for the Eastern District of Washington, 1890–1972* (Washington, DC: National Archives), Record Group 21. Donor information in *Freiheit*, July 4, 1891 through January 20, 1892. Lena Fischer references in *Der deutsche Correspondent* (Baltimore), May 13, May 15, and May 21, 1886; April 5, 1887; November 18, 1887; and January 27, 1890 and in *New York World*, July 28, 1892.

3   Italian anarchist Luigi Lucheni (1873–1910) assassinated Empress Elizabeth of Austria ("Sisi") in Geneva by stabbing her to death as an act of "propaganda by the deed."

4   Leon Frank Czolgosz (1873–1901) was a Michigan-born, Polish-American self-proclaimed anarchist who shot the president at the Pan-American Exposition in Buffalo on September 6, 1901. He was arrested, tried, and executed. McKinley died on September 14. Czolgosz didn't belong to any anarchist group and was not known as an active member in the movement, although Emma Goldman defended his actions. See Goldman, *Emma Goldman: A Documentary History of the American Years, Volume 2: Making Speech Free, 1902–1909*, eds. Candace Falk, Barry Pateman, and Jessica Moran (Urbana: University of Illinois Press, 2005), 517–518.

5   Berkman (1870–1936), also known as "Sasha," was in fact born in the now Lithuanian city of Vilnius (or Vilna when part of the Russian Empire), not Kovno. Berkman shot industrialist Henry Clay Frick on July 23, 1892 as a revolutionary act and in retaliation for Frick's heavy-handed suppression of the Homestead lockout. See Paul Avrich and Karen Avrich, *Sasha and Emma: The Anarchist Odyssey of Alexander Berkman and Emma Goldman* (Cambridge, MA: The Belknap Press of Harvard University Press, 2012), 7, 405. See also Alexander Berkman, *Prison Memoirs of an Anarchist* (New York: Mother Earth Publishing Association, 1912).

6   Emma Goldman, *Living My Life*, vol. 1 (New York: Alfred Knopf, 1931) and vol. 2 (New York: Garden City Publishing Co., 1934).

7   Czar Alexander II was assassinated on March 13, 1881. Two days later, Johann Most delivered a speech celebrating the deed, and on March 19, *Freiheit* appeared with a red band and a front-page article

titled "Endlich!" (or "Finally"). Most was arrested on March 30. On June 26, he was sentenced to sixteen months hard labor.

8   *Fraye Arbeter Shtime* (Free Voice of Labor) was founded in July 1890 as a successor to the weekly *Varhayt* (Truth), the first Yiddish-language anarchist periodical launched in February 1889. Jewish immigrant anarchism in the United States began with the formation of the group Pionire der Frayhayt (Pioneers of Liberty) in the wake of the sentencing of the Haymarket defendants in October 1886. See Paul Avrich, "Jewish Anarchism in the United States," in *Anarchist Portraits* (Princeton, NJ: Princeton University Press, 1990), 176–199.

9   Most was neither Jewish nor Christian, but a self-avowed atheist ever since his adolescent years.

10   Minkin's official given name was almost certainly Helena (meaning "ray of light"). Possibly as a result of her immigration to an urban, multiethnic United States, other versions of her first name were used, such as the anglicized Helen, which Goldman often used. The most common form used by friends and family was Helene (he-le-nuh), a version popular with German-speakers. Her own son, John Jr., insisted on this spelling of his mother's name ("with an 'e' at the end," he told the historian Paul Avrich). Even though Minkin herself uses the formal Helena in her memoir, we have used the more common version Helene. See Paul Avrich interview with John Most, Jr. on October 28, 1979 in Avrich, *Anarchist Voices*, 18.

11   Helene Minkin was born in (1873) and grew up in Grodno (now Hrodna in Belarus). She moved to Bialystok possibly in 1883.

12   In fact, according to the memoir, it was Minkin who managed to furnish Most with the photo after demanding permission from the warden.

13   Minkin gave her birthday as June 10, 1873 on her petition for citizenship. See Minkin's Petition of Citizenship.

14   Goldman wrote: "I knew it would be impossible to sew on a machine in the Minkin flat, it would be too disturbing for everybody. Furthermore, the girls' father had got on my nerves. He was a disagreeable person, never working, and living on his daughters. He seemed erotically fond of Anna, fairly devouring her with his eyes. The more surprising was his strong dislike of Helen, which led to constant quarrelling. At last I decided to move out." See Goldman, *Living My Life*, vol. 1, 37.

15 Goldman wrote: "Our life was active and interesting but presently it was disturbed. Anna, who had been ailing in New York, now grew worse, showing signs of consumption; and one Sunday afternoon, at the close of Most's lecture, Helen became hysterical. There seemed to be no particular cause for her attack, but the next morning she confided to me her love for Most, declaring that she would have to leave for New York, as she could not bear being away from where he was." See Goldman, *Living My Life*, vol. 1, 71–72.

16 World-weariness.

17 Sachs' Café at 31 Norfolk Street off of Grand Street in the heart of the Jewish Lower East Side in New York. [Berkman and Avrich say Suffolk St. in *Sasha and Emma*, 30]. An 1890 New York City directory lists a tobacco store owned by Philip and Meyer Sachs on 31 Norfolk Street. See *The Trow City Directory Co.'s, Formerly Wilson's, Copartnership and Corporation Directory of New York City* (New York: Trow, 1890), 262. See also *Phillips' Business Directory of New York City For 1881–1882* (New York: W. Phillips & Co., 1881), 139, which lists "Sachs, Meyer" as cigar store owner at 311 Bleecker Street.

18 Goldman left Rochester for New York in August 1889 after her breakup with Jacob Kershner, a fellow Russian Jewish worker. They had married in February 1887, but the union was an unhappy one, and Goldman divorced Kershner who begged her to get back together. It was after this second failure that Goldman left Rochester. See Avrich and Avrich, *Sasha and Emma*, 17–18.

19 Isaac Minkin was born in 1853 and became a cantor, a significant synagogue position as music plays a major role in Jewish prayer. Cantors lead prayer alongside the rabbi, and in many cases they were ordained clergy who perform pastoral duties such as weddings. When piecing together several records, it appears that Isaac, who had lost his first wife, remarried. On January 8, 1895, one Isaac Minkin wedded Rosa Ostrowsky Brodsky in Manhattan. Isaac's father is listed as Boris Minkin. Rosa's parents are Jechiel (father) and Steinberg (mother). Rosa was likely much younger than Isaac. The 1910 Census lists Isaac Minkin living with Rosie Minkin in Manhattan's 13th Ward. After Isaac's death, Rosa married Max Herman. In 1958, an obituary for "Rose Herman" appears, in which she is listed as "devoted mother of Helen Most" (stepmother

actually) and passed away in Bronx, NY. See Staatsarchiv Hamburg, *Hamburg Passenger Lists, 1850–1934*, Ancestry.com. Original data: Staatsarchiv Hamburg, Bestand: 373–7 I, VIII (Auswanderungsamt I). See marriage record in "New York, Marriages, 1686–1980," index, *FamilySearch* (https://familysearch.org/pal:/MM9.1.1/ F63D-FQF), Isaac Minkin and Rosa Ostrowsky Brodsky, 08 Jan 1895.]; *1910 United States Federal Census*, Ancestry.com. Original data: *Thirteenth Census of the United States, 1910* (Washington, D.C.: National Archives), Record Group 29. See Rose Herman's obituary in *New York Times*, June 16, 1958.

20   "Fedya" refers to the anarchist artist Modest Aronstam (1871–1958), nicknamed "Modska." Alexander Berkman, in his memoir *Prison Memoirs of an Anarchist*, referred to him as "Fedya." Aronstam arrived in New York in August 1888. He would later leave the anarchist movement to fully embrace his art and changed his name to Modest Stein. See Avrich and Avrich, *Sasha and Emma*, 28–29, 190; see also Paul Avrich's interview with Luba Stein Benenson, Aronstam's daughter, in Avrich, *Anarchist Voices*, 55–56.

21   Emma Goldman arrived in New York a little more than fourteen months after the Minkins did.

22   In fact, only four of the defendants, Albert Parsons, August Spies, Adolph Fischer, and Georg Engel, were executed. Louis Lingg committed suicide in his cell the day before the executions. In June 1893, Illinois Governor John Peter Altgeld pardoned Samuel Fielden, Michael Schwab, and Oscar Neebe.

23   Paul Avrich says the commune residence was a four-room apartment on 42nd Street. See Avrich and Avrich, *Sasha and Emma*, 33.

24   Catherine the Great, Empress of Russia (1729–1796).

25   Emma Goldman was twenty when she arrived in New York City in 1889; Helene Minkin was fifteen or sixteen when they met.

26   In fact, it was Alexander Berkman who was inspired by the fictional character Rakhmetov.

27   Ferdinand Freiligrath (1810–1876) was a German poet and radical agitator who, in 1848, published the poem "Die Revolution." Heinrich Heine (1797–1856), the German Romantic poet composed "The Weaver's Song" (or *Weberlied*, or *Die Weber*) after the suppression of the Silesian weavers' revolt against the state in 1844, a significant moment in the history of worker solidarity in the

early decades of the Industrial Revolution. Ever since his socialist activities in Germany during the early 1870s, Johann Most was composing proletarian songs, which where collected and edited by Gustav Geilhof, and published as *Most's Proletarier-Liederbuch* (Chemnitz: Genossenschafts-Buchdruckerei G. Rübner & Co., 1875). His most enduring song was "Die Arbeitsmänner," still recited by German workers in the twentieth century. In 1888, Most self-published another collection of revolutionary songs, *Sturmvögel. Revolutionäre Lieder und Gedichte* (New York), which is possibly the volume referred to by Minkin. On Most's role as a songwriter, see Werner Hinze, ed. *Johann Most und sein Liederbuch: warum der Philosoph der Bombe Lieder schrieb und ein Liederbuch herausgab (inklusive Liederbuch und Liedanalyse)* (Hamburg: Tonsplitter, 2005).

28 In the fall of 1890, Berkman—with Most's help—arranged to go to New Haven to learn the printer's trade at the *Connecticut Volks-Blatt*, where Paul Gephardt was editor. Soon Goldman, Modest Aronstam ("Fedya"), Anna and Helene Minkin decided to join Berkman. They rented a small house at 25 Silver Street where they sought to recreate their commune. Silver Street no longer exists but was located in the present-day block bounded by Cedar, Amistad, Church, and Columbus Ave. See Avrich and Avrich, *Sasha and Emma*, 41.

29 In his *Prison Memoirs*, in the chapter "The Urge of Sex," Berkman vividly recalls the New Haven days and his passion for Anna Minkin. He uses the following pseudonyms: "The Girl" (Emma Goldman), "The Twin" (Modest "Fedya" Aronstam), "Luba" (Anna Minkin), and "Manya" (Helene Minkin). "We were all in New Haven then [...] The Girl joined me first, for I felt lonely in the strange city, [...] and then came the Twin and Manya. Luba remained in New York; but Manya, devoted little soul, yearned for her sister, and presently the three girls worked side by side in the corset factory. All seemed happy in the free atmosphere, and Luba was blooming into beautiful womanhood. There was a vague something about her that now and then roused in me a fond longing, a rapturous desire." See Berkman, *Prison Memoirs of an Anarchist* (1912; New York: New York Review of Books, 1999), 202.

30 Just before moving to New Haven, Berkman and Aronstam briefly

considered returning to Russia after reading a report in *Century Magazine* about a brutal suppression of a prison uprising in Siberia. See Avrich and Avrich, *Sasha and Emma*, 41.

31   "*Nu*, Helene..." means "Well now, Helene..."

32   It is uncertain who the "abovementioned young man" is. Possibly, this was Anna's future husband or partner with whom she would have a son.

33   Dr. Julius Hoffmann, who lived on 7th Street in New York, was an anarchist physician. He and his wife Ida were close friends of Johann Most (they knew each other since the Berlin days in the 1870s) for whom they posted bail on more than one occasion. He was also a regular financial backer of *Freiheit*, and would occasionally present a lecture on science and the "Ignorance of the 'Learned'" to German anarchists in New York. In the spring of 1889, he undertook a voyage around the world visiting India, China, and Japan and reported on the radical movements there. See *Freiheit*, June 12, 1886; May 4, 1889; January 11, 1890; September 6 and 20, 1890.

34   On June 20, 1891, Johann Most was summoned to serve a prison sentence for a speech he made at Krämer's saloon three-and-a-half years before. On November 12, 1887, the day after four of the Haymarket defendants were hanged, Most thundered against the judicial system and was arrested a few days later. He was found guilty and sentenced to one year on Blackwell's Island (now Roosevelt Island). Most appealed the decision, but in June 1891, his sentence was upheld.

35   Most was released on April 18, 1892.

36   According to John Most Jr., his mother Helene Minkin "though Jewish,...came to believe in the divinity of Jesus and thought that Moses was a tyrant." See interview with John Most Jr., in Avrich, *Anarchist Voices*, 19.

37   April 20, 1892.

38   Goldman wrote: "A home, children, the care and attention ordinary women can give, who have no other interest in life but the man they love and the children they bear him—that was what he needed and felt he had found in Helen." See Goldman, *Living My Life*, vol. 1, 77.

39   She must have immigrated in 1891 since there are no passenger records of her for arrival at Ellis Island, which opened as the new immigrant processing facility in January 1, 1892.

40 Autonomists emerged as a radical faction in anarchism when Austrian anarchist Josef Peukert (1855–1910) and German locksmith Otto Rinke (1853–1899) founded the Autonomy Group (Gruppe Autonomie) in May 1885 in London. Autonomists stressed the freedom of the individual and opposed any form of authority even anarchist federations and labor unions. Specifically, they sought to undermine Most's perceived dominance in the transatlantic movement, and in 1886, they launched *Die Autonomie* as a direct challenge to Most's *Freiheit*. Autonomist groups were formed in the United States, first in Chicago, then St. Louis, northern New Jersey, Brooklyn, and New York. George Engel and Adolph Fischer, two Haymarket anarchists executed in 1887, had been autonomists.

41 Aside from ideological disagreements between Peukert and Most, the two men were personal enemies. Most blamed Peukert for the capture of his friend Johann Christoph Neve (1844–1896) in February 1887 in Belgium. Neve had been in charge of smuggling *Freiheit* and other literature into Germany. Most had no doubt that Peukert informed the authorities, a serious charge that weighed heavily on Peukert. Neve was transferred to an insane asylum in 1892, where he died in December 1896. In May 1887, an investigative committee found no evidence for Most's accusation, but the feud never abated. Peukert immigrated to America in June 1890. In December 1891, at a convention of Yiddish-speaking anarchists, Berkman proposes another committee to resolve the affair, and in November 1894 yet another commission again exonerated Peukert of wrongdoing in the Neve Affair. Most's stubbornness in this affair colored his view of any alternative groups. See Tom Goyens, *Beer and Revolution: The German Anarchist Movement in New York City, 1880–1914* (Urbana: University of Illinois Press, 2007); Rudolf Rocker, *Johann Most: Das Leben eines Rebellen* (Berlin: "Der Syndikalist", 1924; Glashütten im Taunus: Detlov Auvermann, 1973), 340, 353–354; *Der Anarchist* (New York), November 24, 1894; For Peukert's memoirs, see Peukert, *Erinnerungen eines Proletariers aus der revolutionären Arbeiterbewegung* (Verlag des Sozialistischen Bundes, 1913; Frankfurt/M: Verlag Edition AV, 2002). On Neve, see Heiner Becker, "Johann Neve (1844–1896)," *The Raven: Anarchist Quarterly* I, no. 2 (August 1987): 99–114; [Max Nettlau,] "Johann Neve," *Freedom* 113 (February 1897).

42 Johann Most, *Acht Jahre hinter Schloss und Riegel: Skizzen aus dem Leben Johann Most's* (New York: 1886), with new editions in 1887, 1890, and 1891.

43 The Yiddish word *Gemore* refers to part of the Talmud.

44 Bielsk (now Bielsk Podlaski in eastern Poland) is less than thirty miles south of Bialystok and was part of Russia's Grodno Province inside the Pale of Settlement. The 1888 Hamburg ship manifest lists their last place of residence as "Belsk." See Staatsarchiv Hamburg, *Hamburg Passenger Lists, 1850–1934*.

45 Just like the millions of Jews following in the Minkins' footsteps, reaching a transatlantic port from central and Eastern Europe was no easy feat. The majority of Jewish emigrants made their way for ports in northwestern Europe like Hamburg, Bremen, Amsterdam, or Antwerp. Jews living in northwestern Russia, like the Minkins, chose Hamburg, a 650 mile trip from Bialystok. Minkin's memoir is silent about their "journey," for which they began planning in February 1888. She tells us that her father Isaac raised funds, presumably for train fare and steamship tickets. They almost certainly made their way from Bielsk back to Bialystok, which was a railroad hub from where they may have proceeded to Warsaw and on to Prussia to reach Berlin. Legally crossing the border into Germany could also have been an ordeal, although Isaac Minkin may have obtained a passport (elsewhere in her memoir, Minkin mentions a grandparent who worked in St. Petersburg). Undoubtedly, Isaac and his two daughters possessed useful information provided by his brother in New York.

46 They boarded the *SS Wieland* in Hamburg on May 20, 1888. The Wieland was one of the smaller vessels in the Hamburg-Amerika company's fleet. Before crossing the Atlantic, it sailed to the French port of Le Havre, where it picked up some sixty passengers from France and Switzerland. In all, 911 passengers readied themselves for the voyage, nearly all in steerage (only fifty could afford more comfortable quarters), and the vast majority were immigrants from Russia, Germany, Austria, Hungary, Moravia, and Scandinavia. Minkin's petition for citizenship incorrectly lists the name of the vessel of her immigration as *Pocketford* instead of *Wieland*. See *New York, Passenger Lists, 1820–1957*, Ancestry.com. Original data: *Passenger Lists of Vessels Arriving at New York, New York, 1820–1897*

(Washington, D.C.: National Archives), Record Group 36.

47 They arrived on Thursday, May 31, 1888 after an eleven-day voyage. The *Wieland* arrived at the entrance of New York harbor (Sandy Hook Bar) around midday, from whence it was piloted to Castle Garden. See Ancestry.com, *New York, Passenger Lists, 1820–1957.* See also "Marine Intelligence," *New York Daily Tribune,* June 1, 1888.

48 Most was forty-six in 1892.

49 Possibly the Radical Reading Room at number 84, frequented by Yiddish-speaking radicals. There was also Walhalla Hall, a German anarchist saloon located at numbers 45–52. See *Freiheit,* June 1886 and 8 February 1902.

50 Goldman wrote: "Since he [Most] had come out [of prison], he had not asked to see me. I knew he was living with Helen, that she was with child; and I had no right to break in on their life." Goldman, *Living My Life,* 89. In fact, Minkin would become pregnant with her first child in mid-August 1893, and gave birth to John Most Jr. on May 18, 1894.

51 Berkman was transported to the Western Penitentiary of Pennsylvania on September 19, 1892. He was released on July 19, 1905 and transported to the Allegheny County Workhouse to complete a one-year sentence of hard labor. He became a free man on May 18, 1906—after fourteen years behind bars. Johann Most had died two months earlier, on March 17, in Cincinnati.

52 These ideas appeared in Most's article "Attentats-Reflexionen," *Freiheit,* August 27, 1892, in which he reversed his position on political assassinations.

53 Goldman wrote (in response to Most's article): "I wondered if he really believed what he wrote. Was his article prompted by his hatred of Sasha [Berkman], or written to protect himself against the newspaper charge of complicity?" And further: "I replied to his article, in the *Anarchist,* demanding an explanation and branding Most as a traitor and a coward" (Goldman, *Living My Life,* vol. 1, 105). See also her earlier article in *Der Anarchist* (July 30, 1892), in which she attacked Most for being cowardly ("*feig*") and acting out of fear and personal hatred ("*aus Angst und persönlichen Hass*").

54 Minkin refers to financial assistance Goldman received from various people. In 1895, Goldman decided to travel to Europe to acquire medical training to become a licensed nurse. Modest Aronstam paid

for her passage and sent her a monthly allowance of twenty-five dollars to cover expenses. In 1899, Goldman returned to Europe for medical school with generous funding by Herman Miller and Carl Schmidt; they even gave her a gold watch. She never used the money for school, but instead traveled to the major radical centers where she established many contacts. She also sent ten dollars of her funds to her brother Morris. Soon after hearing about this, her funders sent her an angry letter, which she rebuffed; she also pawned the gold watch. In 1904, Goldman started a massage parlor with a loan by Bolton Hall, a prominent lawyer and reformer, which she repaid. Hall also made available a farmhouse near Ossining, New York as a place of relaxation. See Avrich and Avrich, *Sasha and Emma*, 121, 128–9, 146–147, 149–150, 176.

55   Henry Bauer (1861–1934) was a German anarchist and a carpenter by trade, who immigrated in 1880. At the time of Berkman's attempt on Frick's life, Bauer lived at 73 Spring Garden Avenue in Allegheny City, just outside Pittsburgh. See Avrich and Avrich, *Sasha and Emma*, 63.

56   The Elevated railroad, New York City's rapid transit system.

57   This incident happened on December 18, 1892, when Most was to speak at a meeting of a Jewish anarchist group at a hall at 98 Forsyth Street. As Most began to address the crowd, Goldman rose and demanded that Most back up his accusations against Berkman. Most instead mumbled something about a "hysterical woman," upon which Goldman mounted the stage and lashed a horsewhip in his face, then broke the whip over her knee. Goldman and her friends was barely able to escape from the hall. See Goldman, *Living My Life*, vol. 1, 106; Avrich and Avrich, *Sasha and Emma*, 90.

58   There is evidence that Helene Minkin worked for *Freiheit* by the summer of 1891. Her involvement with the paper clearly dates from before Berkman's assassination attempt in July 1892, despite Minkin's chronology in her memoir. In 1891, a Pittsburgh paper reported that Florentina Könnecke went to court because her husband, Wilhelm Könnecke, a long-time friend of Most and distributor of *Freiheit*, had abandoned her. Mrs. Könnecke alleged that her husband illicitly lived with Mrs. Most while Most was in prison. Wilhelm in turn claimed he was not legally married to Florentina and that he stayed at the Most house to help Mrs. Most

with producing *Freiheit*. This "Mrs. Most" could either be Helene Minkin or Lena Fischer since one newspaper reporting on the same court case identified her as "Lena Most." See "An Anarchist Wife," *Pittsburg Dispatch*, September 21, 1891; "Johann Most's Wife Suspected," *New York Tribune*, September 21, 1891.

59 Johann Most was born out of wedlock on February 5, 1846 in his grandfather's house on 225 Lange Sächsen-Gäßchen, an alley in the St. Max parish of Augsburg. His father, Anton Joseph Most (1820–1882) was born in the same house the son of a bricklayer. Most's mother was Viktoria Hinterhuber (1818–1856), a native of Munich and daughter of a staff officer at the Royal Bavarian Ministry of the Army. They were eventually able to marry on October 9, 1848, when Johann Most was two years and eight months old. See *Städtische Polizei, Familienbögen: Most*, Stadtarchiv Augsburg. Anton Joseph Most's birth record in St. Maximilian Geburts-Register 1820, Archiv des Bistums Augsburg. Hinterhuber's birth record in *St. Peter Kirchenbuch* [church book], July 12, 1818. Archiv des Erzbistums München und Freising. On homeowners, see *Verzeichniss der Hausbesitzer in und um Augsburg* (Augsburg: Verlag von J.A. Brinhaußer's Erden, 1844), 74–75.

60 Most, *Memoiren: Erlebtes, Erforschtes und Erdachtes* (New York: Selbstverlag des Verfassers, 1903; Hannover: Edition Kobaia, 1978), I, 10.

61 He contracted the cold at a New Year's Eve party on December 31, 1853. See Most, *Memoiren*, I, 13.

62 Cholera spread to Augsburg in the fall of 1854, possibly coming from Munich. Most's grandmother and grandfather passed away on September 5th and 6th respectively. The epidemic abetted somewhat during the winter, but returned in the spring. In April 1855, Most's two-year-old sister Franziska died, and on May 14, his beloved mother succumbed to the disease. See *Cholera Epidemie 1854 aus den Privat-Papieren des – Comissaer Fiegen*, Magistrat der Stadt Augsburg. Acten. Die Cholera, 1854–1861. Bestand 5, No. 58; *Städtische Polizei, Familienbögen: Most*, Stadtarchiv Augsburg; Most, *Memoiren*, I, 14. Most mistakenly states that the family deaths due to cholera all occurred in 1856.

63 Maria Lederle (1825–1903), daughter of a watchmaker and born in a village less than four miles west of Augsburg and five years Anton's

junior. They married in Augsburg on June 9, 1856. See *Städtische Polizei, Familienbögen: Most*, Stadtarchiv Augsburg.

64   Pauline Most was born in 1849. In 1873, at age twenty-four she was suspected of prostitution by the Munich police. Two years later she was arrested for prostitution this time in Würzburg some 170 miles north of Munich. Eventually, in 1879, she returned to Augsburg and married metalworker Joseph Lieb. See "Verzeichniß anderer zur Familie gehörigen Personen," *Städtische Polizei, Familienbögen: Most*, Stadtarchiv Augsburg.

65   Dr. Georg Joseph Agatz (1821–1894) and his wife Ernestina had come to Augsburg from Würzburg in August 1855, initially to help stem the cholera outbreak. In April 1856, the new physician was appointed "doctor to the poor" (*Armenarzt*) by the city, for district H where the Most residence was located. Agatz told father Most that his son had advanced caries of the left jaw bone (*Knochenfrass*) and needed an operation immediately to save his life. See "Georg Joseph Agatz," Einwohnermeldebogen, Stadtarchiv Würzburg. "Agatz, Georg Jos.," Familien-Bogen, Stadtarchiv Augsburg.

66   The operation took place on March 18, 1859. Most had just turned thirteen. Dr. Agatz and a team of five other physicians worked on him for an hour and fifteen minutes. Five times the boy was anesthetized with chloroform, a common method at the time. First, the surgeons exposed the jawbone by cutting the skin from the left temple to the corner of the mouth. A piece of badly eroded bone about three inches long was removed. Then, the rest of the jawbone was shifted from right to left in order to allow cartilaginification. Agatz would eventually make a name for himself. Only a year after Most's operation, he published an illustrated *Atlas zur chirurgischen Anatomie und Operationslehre* (Atlas of Surgical Anatomy and Operation Training), and later co-authored an influential textbook on children's diseases and methods of surgery. See Most, *Acht Jahre hinter Schloß und Riegel* (New York, 1886), 8. On Agatz' fame, see *De Gids*, 25ste Jaargang 1861, vol. II (Amsterdam: Van Kampen, 1861), 191–192. See also *Hof- und Staatshandbuch des Konigreichs Bayern* (München: Landesamt, 1840), 441.

67   Most played practical jokes on his teachers in retaliation for their reprimands and for the occasional detentions he received for not putting in the effort. Most freely admits to bringing snuff tobacco

to school, an explicit violation of the school code of conduct. He also attempted to orchestrate a class strike against his French teacher Félix Bourier, who had imposed a class-wide punishment, although Most does not specify what that was. See Most, *Memoiren*, I, 18.

68   In the spring of 1860, at age fourteen, Johann Most was apprenticed to master bookbinder Johann Jakob Weber, who lived at 13 Mittlerer Lech, halfway between Most's house and the central Rathausplatz (Town Hall Square). See *Adressbuch der Königlichen Kreishauptstadt Augsburg. nach amtl. Quellen zusammengestellt* (Augsburg, 1862), 207.

69   Johann Most said goodbye to his father and left Augsburg on April 21, 1863, heading for Frankfurt.

70   This episode occurred in May 1866, when Most found work in Tessin, a village seventeen miles east of Rostock near the Baltic Sea. It is unclear if he worked for a bookbinder, but one A. Kloß lived in town around this time. His friendship with his master ended in June 1866 with the outbreak of a civil war between Prussia, Italy, and their German allies, against Austria and its German allies. The economy went into recession across Germany as demand for luxury goods such as books and leather cases bottomed out. Most was forced to move on. See Most, *Memoiren*, I, 48; *Archiv für Landeskunde in den Grossherzogthümern Mecklenburg*, vol. 18 (Schwerin: Sandmeyer, 1868), 247.

71   A court in Vienna convicted Most and three other activists of treason on July 19, 1870. He received a sentence of five years, but it was later reduced to three. The trial was the culmination of Most's activities in the budding socialist movement in Austria from October 1868, when he arrived in the Habsburg Empire, until May 1871, when he was expelled. Most never served the full sentence; a newly installed Austrian government amnestied all political prisoners in February 1871. See Heinrich Scheu, ed, *Der Hochverratsprozeß gegen Oberwinder, Andr. Scheu, Most, Papst, Hecker, Perrin, Schönfelder, Berka, Schäftner, Pfeiffer, Dorsch, Eichinger, Gehrke, und Baudisch. Verhandelt vor dem k. k. Landesgerichte in Wien begonnen am 4. Juli 1870. Nach stenographischen Berichten bearbeitet und herausgegen von Heinrich Scheu* (Wien: Selbstverlag, 1870).

72   Most's letter appears in full in the trial transcript of Scheu, ed. *Der Hochverratsprozeß*, 241. Most uses the more formal German *"Sie"*

(You) to address his father, as Minkin observes as well.

73   Part of the friction with his father stemmed from the fact that Anton Joseph Most had become a staunch Roman Catholic and may have espoused ultramontanism (from the Latin *ultra montes*, across the mountains, or Alps), an anti-modern political current in Germany and the Low Countries that strictly followed papal authority. He could not understand why his son had embraced socialism.

74   In fact, his travels through Austria, Hungary, and Italy occurred during the 1860s. After his expulsion from Austria in 1871, Most headed to Saxony after a brief sojourn in Bavaria.

75   From the summer of 1871 until December 1878, Most lived in Chemnitz, Mainz, and Berlin.

76   In July 1871 while in Chemnitz, Most met nineteen-year-old Clara Franziska Hänsch, a policeman's daughter. On June 21 or 22, 1874, Most and Hänsch married in Bischofsheim near Mainz in Hessen. In October, their first son was born, but died a few weeks later. On May 9, 1878, a daughter Melita Clara was born, but she also died six months later. See Most, *Memoiren*, III, 27, 28; *Städtische Polizei, Familienbögen: Most*, Stadtarchiv Augsburg. On Melita, see *Acta des Königlichen Polizei-Präsidii zu Berlin betreffend den Johann Most, 1874–80*, A. Br; Pr. 030, Landesarchiv Berlin, 2.

77   This refers to Most's trial and conviction in England in 1881 for printing an article praising the assassination of Czar Alexander II. Most was sentenced to sixteen months (not twenty-six) in Clerkenwell Prison. He was released on October 25, 1882. Most had traveled to London in December 1878, and Clara joined him shortly thereafter. Their relationship was already strained, and finally they divorced in the summer of 1880. A few months later, Hänsch married Wilhelm Wentker, a rival of Most within the exile socialist movement in London. Clara Hänsch died in January 1883, about a month after Most arrived in New York. See Heiner Becker, "Johann Most," in *Internationale wissenschaftliche Korrespondenz zur Geschichte der deutschen Arbeiterbewegung* vol. 41, no. 1–2, (Mar 2005): 27, note 89. On Hänsch's death, see *Süddeutsche Post*, (Munich), January 24, 1883.

78   This may refer to Franz Josef Ehrhart (1853–1908), a close friend of Most's, who was living in London for years when Most arrived. It was Ehrhart who suggested founding a new organ in London, with Most

as editor. See Ehrhart, "Aus meiner Londoner Zeit. Erinnerungen,"
Der Neue Welt Kalender für das Jahr 1908, vol. 32 (Hamburg,
1908): 58–62 and Ehrhart, "Die Gründung der "Freiheit," *Vorwärts*
(Berlin: March 14, 1924), Abendausgabe.

79   In fact, he served one prison term in England.

80   Most had intended to move to the United States in December 1878
after his release from a Berlin prison. He made his way to London in
order to move on across the Atlantic, but was persuaded by his friend
Franz Josef Ehrhart to stay and launch a new socialist newspaper.
After a few years in London, on December 1, 1882, Most traveled
to Liverpool. The next day, he boarded the *SS Wisconsin* of the
Guion Line at the "intermediate" rate of passage (steerage being
the cheapest, cabin the costliest). He was the only German among
a total of 144 passengers. He arrived in New York on December
18, a cold winter day, and was greeted by several members of a new
social-revolutionary club. The ship's manifest listed his name as "Jno.
Moest." See Ancestry.com. *New York, Passenger Lists, 1820–1957*.

81   At 167 William Street in lower Manhattan.

82   Minkin refers to the Haymarket affair of 1886–1887.

83   Most had already been charged, then arrested and sentenced in New
York for an incendiary speech he made on April 23, 1886 at a meeting
of a German anarchist rifle club, in which he urged workers to arm
themselves instead of advocating for an eight-hour day. New York
authorities refused to extradite him. See Henry David, *History of the
Haymarket Affair: A Study of the American Social-Revolutionary and
Labor Movements* (New York: Farrar & Rinehart, 1936), 168.

84   Before moving to Brooklyn, Most and Minkin possibly lived in a
three-story tenant apartment at 266 William Street near *Freiheit's*
editorial office at 166 William Street in Manhattan. According to
reports, "Lizzie Most, the reputed wife of John Most," as the papers
called her, contracted smallpox there and had to be removed to
Riverside Hospital on North Brother Island in the East River. See
New York Tribune, October 16, 1893. The Brooklyn address is
unclear. In December 1893, a notice appeared in the *Brooklyn Daily
Eagle*, stating that "five or six weeks ago" Most moved into a house
on Skillman Ave not far from Lorimer Street in the Williamsburg
section of Brooklyn. Perhaps less believable, the report stated that
"sometimes he is accompanied by a richly dressed woman," and that

"it is said" Most "has been negotiating for the purchase of the house where he now resides, and possibly is already its owner." See "Most in Brooklyn. The Anarchist Leader Now a Resident of the Fifteenth Ward," *Brooklyn Daily Eagle*, December 18, 1893.

85   Louise Michel (1830–1905) was a French revolutionary and leader during the 1871 Paris Commune, calling on workers to arm themselves. She was deported to New Caledonia and became an anarchist. Upon her return to France in 1880, she continued her revolutionary activities, giving speeches, leading demonstrations, and attending the 1881 London anarchist congress.

86   We found information for only two previous children.

87   Most traveled to Chicago in early November 1894 to speak at the Haymarket memorial in Waldheim Cemetery. Apparently a train with some 1,500 anarchists wrecked in Chicago causing one fatality (the engineer) and several injured. It is unclear if Most was also on that train. In March 1895, he addressed a crowd in Orpheus Hall in Cleveland to raise funds for *Freiheit*. See "Anarchists' Train Wrecked in Chicago," *New York Times*, November 12, 1894; *Brooklyn Daily Eagle*, March 31, 1895.

88   Lucifer Most was born July 22, 1895.

89   Johann Most died at the age of sixty on March 17, 1906.

90   Shabby garments.

91   [Translator's Note] "Kibbetzernye" is American Yiddish slang for a place frequented by those who like to banter, mock, joke around. A place for kibbetzers.

92   In fact, the *Buffaloer Arbeiter-Zeitung* already existed since September 11, 1887 and would fold on February 2, 1918. The offer from Buffalo was that the *Arbeiter-Zeitung* publishers assume ownership of *Freiheit*, but allow it to continue to appear as a weekly with Most as editor. This publishing arrangement lasted from September 18, 1897 until July 1898 when Most returned to New York City.

93   Most moved to Buffalo on September 7, 1897. The *Freiheit* situation was indeed dire. The *Tribune* reported that his paper had not appeared since August 7. Friends and comrades organized an outdoor farewell gathering on the 6th in a Fort Wadsworth, Staten Island park. See "New York to Lose Herr Most," *New York Tribune*, September 1, 1897; "Herr Most's Last Day Here," *New York Times*,

September 7, 1897.

94 He undertook a fundraising trip to the West coast. He arrived in San Francisco on December 17, 1899 and stayed until February, when he traveled to Seattle. See *San Francisco Call*, December 19, 1899; *Yakima Herald*, February 8, 1900.

95 Hillel Solotaroff (1865–1921) was a Russian-born physician and Yiddish-speaking anarchist lecturer and writer. See Goldman, *Emma Goldman: A Documentary History of the American Years. Volume 1: Made for America, 1890–1901*, ed. by Candace Falk, Barry Pateman, Jessica Moran (Berkeley: University of California Press, 2003), 556.

96 According to their oldest son John Jr., Helene Minkin had an affair with August L. Lott (1872–1934) while Most was alive. Lott was a young activist, speaker, and loyal follower of Most. In 1890, he was active in Cincinnati and then Chicago. At the beginning of 1895, Lott moves to New York to serve as collector for *Freiheit*. At a 1908 May Day demonstration, Lott praised the Jewish anarchists for being more committed to the cause than the Germans who seem to prefer sitting in their clubrooms. See Paul Avrich interview with John Most, Jr. on October 28, 1979 in Avrich, *Anarchist Voices*, 19; on Lott see *Freiheit*, September 27, 1890; November 22, 1890; February 23, 1895; May 9, 1908. See also "United States Census, 1930," index and images, *FamilySearch* (https://familysearch.org/pal:/MM9.1.1/X745-JJF : accessed 28 Jul 2013), August Lott, 1930. In 1904, Emma Goldman also refers to an affair Helene Minkin had with the German actor Josef Jülich. In a letter to Berkman, Goldman writes, "She [Helene] has not left the pope [Most] but she has some affaire [sic] with another beastly speciemen [sic] of the male sex [Jülich], although much younger than papa [Most] and phisically [*sic*] superior still a very inferior Man otherwise *ein Kaffer und Waschweib* [an idiot and a gossip] par Excellence." See Emma Goldman to Alexander Berkman, New York, ca. February 21, 1904, in Goldman, *Emma Goldman: A Documentary History of the American Years, Volume 2*, 137. On Jülich as actor, see *Freiheit*, October 17, 1896.

97 Abe and Mary Isaak were pacifist Mennonites who in 1889 moved to Oregon from Ekaterinoslav (now Dnepropetrovsk in the Ukraine). They published *The Firebrand* and later in San Francisco

renamed it *Free Society* in which they advocated free love and gender equality. *Free Society* also played an important role in introducing the philosophy of anarchist communism to American activists. They moved to Chicago in 1900, and later to the Bronx. See Goyens, *Beer and Revolution*, 195–199.

98 Evgenii Nikolayevich Chirikov (1864–1932) was a Russian writer, dramatist, and publicist. As a student at Kazan University, he joined a revolutionary group and was arrested several times for publishing anti-czarist material. One of his most imporant plays was *Evrei* (The Jews) from 1904, although in America the play was known as *The Chosen People*. In the spring of 1905, Pavel Orleneff and Alla Nazimova arrived in New York with their dramatic company, opening with this Chirikov play on March 23rd at the Herald Square Theater. Emma Goldman acted as manager for the company. The Kishinev pogrom, one of the first atrocities of the twentieth century, occurred on April 6 and 7, 1903, when mob violence against the Jewish community caused forty-nine deaths. See Moses Rischin, *The Promised City: New York's Jews, 1870–1914* (Cambridge: Harvard University Press, 1962), 137; "Kishineff's Horrors Shown," *The [New York] Sun*, March 24, 1905. Goldman, *Emma Goldman: A Documentary History of the American Years. Volume 2*, 33–34.

99 [Translator's Note] Literally "Jewish head."

100 [Translator's Note] Literally "Gentile head."

101 John Most, Jr. admired his father but hardly ever saw him, "as he lectured and traveled all over and was very busy with his paper, *Freiheit*..." Home life was difficult. "There were so many tragedies in our life. And my parents did not get along [...] Mother was too young for him; she was nineteen and he forty-six or forty-seven when they got together [...] In Father's last years things became worse and worse between them. He was growing old and getting impatient. They quarreled and threw pots and pans at each other when my brother and I were babies. Mother, I think, was unfair to him. She should have been more tolerant." See interview with John Most, Jr., in Avrich, *Anarchist Voices*, 18–19.

102 On September 5, the day before the shooting, *Freiheit* came out with an 1849 article "Mord contra Mord" (Murder against Murder) by the German radical Karl Heinzen (1809–1880) in which he justified the murder of murderers. Most briefly remarked that the

author's views "are still true today." See Avrich and Avrich, *Sasha and Emma*, 164.

103   Most was arrested on September 22, 1901 during an anarchist meeting in Corona, Queens for inciting to riot, although he had appeared before a magistrate on the 16th. See "John Most is Again Arrested," *New York Times*, September 23, 1901; "Johann Most's Bond Reduced," *New York Times*, September 17, 1901.

104   Most was convicted and sentenced on October 14, 1901 in the Court of Special Sessions. His lawyer filed an appeal. Most was released on bail on October 30.

105   Most's attorney was the celebrated labor lawyer and socialist Morris Hillquit (1869–1933).

106   According to the New York dailies, at the time of the trial, Most resided at 375 15th Street, Brooklyn. See *New York Times*, September 13, 1901; *New York Tribune*, September 13, 1901. The 1900 census, enumerated on June 7, lists Most and Minkin living with their two sons at 434 13th Street (22nd Ward) in Brooklyn, a block from Prospect Park. See: Ancestry.com, *1900 United States Federal Census*, Brooklyn Ward 22, Kings, New York; Roll T623_1059; Page 10A; Enumeration District 366.

107   John Most Jr. recalled their poor existence in "a series of basement apartments on the Lower East Side," and that "the neighbors threw insults—and sometimes rocks—at us: 'There go the filthy anarchists!' 'There's that anarchist rat family!' We were abused continually. Even now, in my old age, I'm occasionally accosted; once this happened in a neighborhood supermarket, where someone called me a 'dirty anarchist.'" See interview with John Most, Jr., in Avrich, *Anarchist Voices*, 18.

108   The Court of Appeals in Albany, NY denied Most's appeal on April 29, 1902 and confirmed his earlier conviction and sentencing on June 10; Most was to serve one year in prison. See "John Most Must Go to Prison," *New York Times*, April 30, 1902; "Most's Sentence Affirmed," *New York Times*, June 11, 1902.

109   They all went to court on June 20, 1902. August Albinger (1851–1903) owned a lager beer saloon at 3465 Third Ave, between 167th and 168th Streets in the Bronx. He was a close friend of Most and supporter of *Freiheit*. See his obituary in *Freiheit*, March 7, 1903.

110   A *Times* reporter heard Most shout "This is the funeral day of the

freedom of the American press!" He then "broke down and sobbed as the court officers hurried him from the room." But as he was escorted away, "his wife, sitting in the last row of the benches, jumped to her feet, threw her arms out and caught the weeping Anarchist. She kissed him frantically, and then the officers pushed him ahead of them," See "A Year in Prison For Most," *New York Times*, June 21, 1902.

111   Ahasuerus is the Biblical name for the Persian king Xerxes.

112   Most was released from prison in the first week of April 1903. On April 11, he was welcomed at a large reception in Progress Hall (28–30 Avenue A) with several bands and singing groups before he delivered the keynote speech. The festivities were overshadowed by the death of Edward Brady, the Austrian anarchist, who had passed away on April 2. See "Zur John Most Empfangs-Feier," *Freiheit*, April 4, 1903; Brady's obituary in *Freiheit*, April 11, 1903.

113   This should be 26th street pier. Ferries from Blackwell's Island to Manhattan stopped at the foot of 116th, 70th, 52nd, and 26th streets.

114   This is a curious error. Most was released in April 1903. Presumably, Minkin is referring to the Hippodrome Theater, located on Sixth Avenue between West 43rd and West 44th Streets, but this building, claimed to be the largest theater in the world, seating 5,300, opened on April 12, 1905. It is possible she referred to the circular hippodrome within the Luna Park complex in Coney Island, but Luna Park opened on May 16, 1903, a month after Most's reunion with Minkin and his sons. Thanks to the New York Historical Society for this information.

115   Likely this didn't happen after his 1903 release. Minkin herself mentions below that Most published or wrote his second pamphlet shortly after the McKinley shooting in 1901. Rudolf Rocker believes Most published the first volume of his memoirs in the spring of 1902. However, ads for the sale of his first volume (at 25 cents) started to appear in *Freiheit* in June 1903; the second volume's publication was anticipated for the end of that month. See Rocker, *Johann Most*, 412; *Freiheit*, June 20, 1903.

116   This is Most's sixtieth birthday on February 5, 1906.

117   This may have been the meeting on March 10, 1906, broken up by police. The gathering was organized to celebrate Most's sixtieth birthday. He began to speak about his life, then police entered and

ordered him to stop. He complied. The hall was cleared but no arrests were made. See "Drive Out Anarchists," *New York Tribune*, March 11, 1906.

118 *Freiheit* was printed by F.W. Heiss at 465 Pearl Street. Perhaps Minkin inadvertently anglicized his name to "Hayes." It is less likely that Minkin refers to Timothy J. Hayes, owner of Hayes Printing Co. located in 1909 at 242 W 41st Street. See *The Trow (formerly Wilson's) Copartnership and Corporation Directory of New York City* (New York: Trow, 1909), 337.

119 Johann Joseph Most died at the age of sixty on Saturday, March 17, 1906 in the house of his friend Emil Krause at 1525 Cutter Street in Cincinnati (not Adolph Krause as was reported); Minkin was thirty-two at the time of his death. The cause of death was reported to be an attack of erysipelas, a bacterial infection of the upper dermis appearing as a red, swollen rash. Most had lately been suffering from frequent fevers, chills, and fatigue, all common symptoms of the disease. The disease mainly occurred in the winter months, and March typically saw the most cases. It was generally not fatal unless someone had been weakened by other ailments. Penicillin, not discovered until 1928, may have cured this condition. A *Sun* reporter wrote that Dr. Joseph Meitus, a graduate of the University of Cincinnati, attended Most and "said he died without a struggle." See "Johann Most Dead After Brief Illness," *New York Times*, March 18, 1906; "Most, the Anarchist, Dead," *The [New York] Sun*, March 18, 1906. Krause's address was listed as "apt h 1523 Cutter" in *Williams' Cincinnati Directory* (Cincinnati, June 1906), 1009. Becker, "Johann Most," 61.

120 These costs were defrayed through fundraising. Minkin's trip to Cincinnati ($55) was made possible through Heiss (the same printer whom Minkin may have named "Hayes"). Telephone and telegram charges between Cincinnati and New York ($2.65) were also taken care of. See expense report for Most's memorial in *Freiheit*, April 28, 1906.

121 Most's body was cremated in Cincinnati on March 20. Apparently, the New York comrades thought the amount of ashes Minkin brought with her too small. More than three years later the *New York Times* reported that a friend found a "bottle in the Krause home which contained ashes and bore the sign, 'Ashes of Herr

Johann Most." Krause had kept some of it as a souvenir and never told Minkin. See Rocker, *Johann Most*, 428; "Kept Herr Most's Ashes," *New York Times*, August 22, 1909.

122   Emma Goldman wrote: "We [Goldman and Max Baginski] were both asked to speak. I was informed that the invitation to me had been protested against by some of Most's supporters, especially his wife, who considered it 'sacrilegious' for Emma Goldman to pay tribute to Johann Most. I had no desire to intrude, but the younger comrades in the German ranks, as well as many of the Yiddish anarchists, insisted on my speaking." See Goldman, *Living My Life*, vol. 1, 380.

123   At the end of her letter, Minkin states her desire to edit and publish Most's papers, and that anyone interested in such a project should contact her. While much of Most's writings have been published (mostly in German), it is to this day unknown where (or whether) any personal papers or other material may exist. See Minkin's "An die Leser der 'Freiheit,'" *Freiheit*, April 21, 1906.

124   On April 22, 1906, a day after Minkin's letter, a general meeting was held at a beerhall on East 80th Street (Manhattan) to work out a plan to keep *Freiheit* going (against the wishes of Minkin who relinquished all "liabilities" with the paper). The paper continued to appear under the leadership of a new Freiheit Publishing Association. Max Baginski took over as editor in January 1908. The paper folded for good on August 17, 1910. See "An die Leser und Freunde der 'Freiheit,'" *Freiheit*, April 28, 1906.

125   A 1910 city directory lists one "Helen V. Miller" as having a "manicure" business at 162 West 66th Street. See *Trow's General Directory of the Boroughs of New York and Bronx, City of New York* (New York, 1910), vol 2, 1007.

126   John Most, Jr. would be eighteen, and presumably graduating in 1912; Lucifer in 1913.

INDEX

Support **AK Press!**

AK Press is one of the world's largest and most productive anarchist publishing houses. We're entirely worker-run &

democratically managed. We operate without a corporate structure—no boss, no managers, no bullshit. We publish close to twenty books every year, and distribute thousands of other titles published by other like-minded independent presses and projects from around the globe.

The Friends of AK program is a way that you can directly contribute to the continued existence of AK Press, and ensure that we're able to keep publishing great books just like this one! Friends pay $25 a month directly into our publishing account ($30 for Canada, $35 for international), and receive a copy of every book AK Press publishes for the duration of their membership! Friends also receive a discount on anything they order from our website or buy at a table: 50% on AK titles, and 20% on everything else. We've also added a new Friends of AK ebook program: $15 a month gets you an electronic copy of every book we publish for the duration of your membership. Combine it with a print subscription, too!

There's great stuff in the works—so sign up now to become a Friend of AK Press, and let the presses roll!

Won't you be our friend? Email friendsofak@akpress.org for more info, or visit the Friends of AK Press website: www.akpress.org/programs/friendsofak